EAT
PEOPLE

EAT
PEOPLE

*and Other Unapologectic
Rules for Game-Changing
Entrepreneurs*

ANDY KESSLER

PORTFOLIO / PENGUIN

PORTFOLIO / PENGUIN
Published by the Penguin Group
Penguin Group (USA) Inc., 375 Hudson Street, New York, New York 10014, U.S.A.
Penguin Group (Canada), 90 Eglinton Avenue East, Suite 700, Toronto, Ontario,
Canada M4P 2Y3 (a division of Pearson Penguin Canada Inc.); Penguin Books
Ltd, 80 Strand, London WC2R 0RL, England; Penguin Ireland, 25 St. Stephen's
Green, Dublin 2, Ireland (a division of Penguin Books Ltd); Penguin Books
Australia Ltd, 250 Camberwell Road, Camberwell, Victoria 3124, Australia (a
division of Pearson Australia Group Pty Ltd); Penguin Books India Pvt Ltd, 11
Community Centre, Panchsheel Park, New Delhi – 110 017, India; Penguin Group
(NZ), 67 Apollo Drive, Rosedale, North Shore 0632, New Zealand (a division of
Pearson New Zealand Ltd); Penguin Books (South Africa) (Pty) Ltd, 24 Sturdee
Avenue, Rosebank, Johannesburg 2196, South Africa

Penguin Books Ltd, Registered Offices:
80 Strand, London WC2R 0RL, England

First published in 2011 by Portfolio / Penguin,
a member of Penguin Group (USA) Inc.

10 9 8 7 6 5 4 3 2 1

LIBRARY OF CONGRESS CATALOGING IN PUBLICATION DATA
Kessler, Andy.
    Eat people : unapologetic rules for entrepreneurial success / Andy Kessler.
        p. cm.
    Includes index.
    ISBN 978-1-59184-377-1
    1. Entrepreneurship.   2. Technological innovations—Economic aspects.
    3. New products.   4. Value.   5. Economics.   I. Title.
    HB615.K396 2011
    658.4'09—dc22   2010039727

Printed in the United States of America
Set in Minion
Designed by Lucy Albanese

To Brett, Ryan, Kurt, and Kyle.
I wrote this for you.

CONTENTS

BONUS RULE

EAT
PEOPLE

Something from Nothing

I'VE SEEN IT HAPPEN SO MANY TIMES.

Someone comes up with a great idea and changes the world.

The next big thing.

I met Michael Dell by phone in his dorm room where he was selling PCs and then met him in person well before Dell Inc. completely changed how personal computers were sold. By getting rid of an entire swath of middlemen, and lowering prices for all of us, he turned himself into a multibillionaire.

I met Steve Jobs as he was getting thrown out of Apple, and once more as he headed back in, when he expanded the company's mission from designing computers to MP3 players and then smart phones and tablets that have made it easier for all of us to get information by voice or by Web wherever we might find ourselves. He got rich—and you and I got richer lives.

I met Ed Catmull while sitting on the floor at LAX waiting for a delayed flight back to SFO. Pixar was working on its first feature film, *Toy Story*, which pioneered a whole new way to tell compelling stories. He (and Steve Jobs) got rich, but the rest of us got to see spectacular movies for ten bucks. Quite the bargain.

I met Carl Rosendahl, whose Pacific Data Images was doing similar things for Jeffrey Katzenberg and DreamWorks with a project called *Shrek*.

I met Larry Ellison as he was selling databases to corporations, when it wasn't so obvious that he was going to completely transform their back offices, squeezing out costs in their finance and supply chains and making them much more productive. Oracle saved businesses a fortune, and they passed the savings along to the rest of us in the form of everything from cheap goods at Walmart to cheap trades at Charles Schwab. Sure, Larry got rich—after all, he saved these companies a ton of money. But he made the rest of us rich, too. As costs go down, all of us get wealthier.

I've met Bill Gates many times, first after Microsoft went public. Gates was pitching Wall Street about upgrading to Windows from DOS (without much luck). Eventually, Wall Street discovered spreadsheets, which lowered their costs and made it vastly easier to do things like take two companies or two financial instruments and merge them into something financeable.

I met Gordon Moore and Andy Grove and Bob Noyce, the founders of Intel, just as they almost lost out to cheap Japanese memory makers—before turning the massive company on a dime to sell processors (at high margins) to the IBMs and Compaqs and then Dells of the world, driving faster and faster computers so better and better graphics could make computers easier to use for business and making all of us more productive—well, except for those of us who love video games.

I heard Sergey Brin and Larry Page speak to a small group a few years before Google went public. They wanted to know what you were going to search for before you even knew yourself.

I met Rupert Murdoch in the early nineties when he almost lost News Corporation under a siege of debt, and when he began transforming the entire media space, from newspapers to TV to film.

I met Mark Cuban when he and his partner Todd Wagner were peddling AudioNet to anyone in Silicon Valley who would listen, before they sold the audio and video streaming company to Yahoo! for $5.7 billion.

I met Mark Zuckerberg just as Facebook was crossing a few million users; he talked about lowering the cost of communications between groups of people. Today, a good chunk of the planet logs in to the site regularly to keep in touch with friends and family.

I can go on. Meg Whitman when she was at eBay, Jeff Bezos at Amazon, even a few telecom folks who were billionaires for a moment in time.

The cool thing about all these folks is that no one did them any favors. There was no government contract that guaranteed them success. No secret handshakes or sweetheart deals or smoky room concessions.

For the most part, society didn't do them any favors—each of them started small, but saw something big on the horizon and created a process to constantly improve, constantly innovate, and constantly sell exactly what was needed and then identify the next big thing on the new horizon.

Wouldn't you like to have their vision?

How do you find the next big thing?

Yeah, sure, none of them discovered penicillin or cured polio. But these folks increased my standard of living, your standard of living, half the world's standard of living, on par with any scientist or philanthropist. They created wealth for themselves, yes, but also for society as a whole, by making all of us more productive.

You can too.

So, HOW WAS I lucky enough to meet all these folks?

Well, it was my job. I worked on Wall Street trying to find the next big things.

I started out as an engineer, designing computer chips and writing software, but I wasn't all that good at it. I spent too much time dreaming about what could be done with all this newfangled technology rather than inventing it.

Luckily, I tripped across a job on Wall Street analyzing those who did do a good job at it. Best thing that happened to me.

I was an analyst tracking the technology business and it was my job to figure out which tech companies and which entrepreneurs would hit it big so mutual funds and pension funds and individuals could invest in them. The best way to do this was to think out, envision, heck, even hallucinate the next big thing, and then find all the companies that were in the right place to make it happen.

I was an investment banker—until I found out you had to be nice to people—trying to figure out which companies would be growing so fast that they would need to raise tons of capital to support their growth.

I was a venture capitalist, investing in entrepreneurs and start-ups that might go from nothing to something to the next big thing attacking these future markets. The only way to do that well was to figure out what really was going to happen next.

And then I ran a hedge fund. My partner Fred Kittler and I

invested in public companies and private companies that we thought would benefit from the next set of big trends. Getting the company right or wrong was hard enough, but if we didn't get the trend right, we would lose real people real money, with our fingerprints all over it.

So yeah, it really was my job to find billionaires well before they hit it big so my investors and I could go along for the ride. And I made tons of mistakes, believe me. But eventually, I got good at it. It was not just finding driven people with the character and focus and guts to succeed. It was also about being in the right zip code, finding the next big applications and companies and industries well before they took off, when you could invest on the cheap and then sell when they were dear.

Along the way, I learned that those things that made me the most money were not so coincidentally the very same things that made society richer and the world a better place.

WHY AM I telling you all this?

Because you really can do this too. I made it out alive and with my reputation intact because I sat down and figured out what works and what doesn't, what turns ideas into monster markets and huge growth trends, and what peters out.

I don't care about and certainly don't idolize those billionaires, beyond what I've learned from them about how to find and create and leverage the next big things.

I don't do this because I'm such a nice guy or can't help but share some of my secret sauce. It's purely selfish. I want you to invent or help invent or even mop the floors for those who invent the future, coming up with the next set of great tools and gadgets and productive services. The more you do, the better off we all are. So sure, I'll fill you in on what works.

But I've got to tell you—if all you want to do is take over some old-line company and milk it for all it's worth, I can't help you. Or if you insist on pursuing some protected franchise in banking or insurance or medicine or whatever—forget it, you're on your own. You may get rich milking the rest of us, but society won't get rich along with you.

But if you want to make something for nothing, help the world be more productive, create wealth for the masses beyond anyone's imagination . . . I can steer you in the right direction whether you're an entrepreneur or an investor or just looking for the right career.

Just be warned. This is not some get-rich-quick scheme. You won't find tips on flipping properties in these pages. What I'm talking about is a process that works over years and decades to keep generating wealth for those who sell and those who buy. And that is what generates progress. And wealth.

I know. I've seen it happen. As I said, I've gone along for the ride many times.

Musée

"THIS PLACE IS SPECTACULAR."

It was, but I wasn't about to let on.

"Amazing." I stifled a yawn.

"And the artwork is something else," Nancy, my wife, continued. "Now this is the way to live."

Paris is one of my favorite places in the world—one giant museum. The food, the wine, the artwork; even the people are nice, some of them anyway. After a quick connection with the gargoyles at Notre Dame—one of them reminds me of a kid I went to high school with—it was time to find things my wife Nancy and I hadn't seen before. No fan of wandering through trendy neighborhoods or doing mindless shopping, I hit on the idea of visiting a bunch of the smaller museums, set in once private homes like the Frick Museum in New York. Frick made his money turning coal into coke for making steel, later hooking up with Carnegie to form what would become U.S. Steel. He deserved a nice house.

My ploy worked, so it was off to Boulevard Haussmann and some wealthy dead French guy's house stuffed with beautiful paintings and sculptures and furnishings—the Jacquemart-André or the Cognacq-Jay. Or the André Jay?

"And over here is the living room, where formal entertaining for the close associates of Monsieur . . ." the guide droned on.

I could see a plate on a side table inscribed with "Liberté, Égalité, Fraternité." How very French. I was starting to go stir crazy. It was time to mix it up.

"Where are the speakers?" I whispered to Nancy.

"What?"

"Some nice B&O speakers and a decent subwoofer would do this room just right. Even just a PC running iTunes, or geez, at least a measly iPod." She shushed me.

"Look at that carpet," she suggested. "Hand woven, I'll bet."

"This rug's from Persia," I said, doing my best Eddie Murphy from the movie *Trading Places*. "But who cleans that? Do you think he had a Dirt Devil?"

"Be nice."

"If you'll step this way, we enter the family living quarters. This drawing room is where the family spent evenings, reading by candlelight, telling stories . . ."

"You could probably shoehorn a nice fifty-two-inch plasma over that dresser. I wonder if they had DirecTV then? If not, I wouldn't want to be this guy."

"Shhhhh."

"The bureau is a Louis XV, and the chairs are quite appropriate for the time period."

"They look really uncomfortable," I remarked. "You think they recline?"

"Would you be quiet?" Nancy said with a laugh. "I don't know you." I finally had her in the right spirit.

"The air conditioning bills must have been killer, at least five hundred a month."

"Stop."

"I can't. This guy has some nice art on the walls, but I wouldn't trade places with him for even a second."

"But he was an elite in Paris during their golden age," Nancy cooed.

"He's got nothing. I haven't seen one Blu-ray player, let alone a refrigerator, toaster oven, or espresso machine." I was on a roll. Why stop there? "If he had a garage, it smelled like horseshit, instead of sporting a four-hundred-horsepower, seven-passenger Suburban. How could he get to his country home in a couple of hours? It must have taken a full day in a carriage. And we flew here in nine hours on a 777—it would have taken him nine months to get to California. I guarantee he never made it for a visit."

"Yeah, but . . ."

"But nothing. This guy was poor. No computer, no Internet, no search engine, no YouTube videos. This guy has never seen *Star Wars*, for God's sake!"

"That's living?"

"Damn right. Should I go on?"

"Don't."

"Cell phone. GPS. Xbox. World of Warcraft. Métro. And," I paused to catch my breath, "I can almost guarantee *le dude* never used Twitter."

I got the eye roll from Nancy. I was pushing this beyond the point of no return.

"Let alone antibiotics, stents for heart attacks—he either died young of tuberculosis or, worse, watched as one of his kids died young. This guy was one of the richest in the world but he'd be considered living under the poverty line in our day."

"I'm going to the next museum by myself."

THE EXPERIENCE GOT me thinking. I've been around the investment business for way too many years, trying to understand business cycles and product cycles, assessing management, picking stocks that go up, avoiding those that go down, but it wasn't until I gawked my way through Monsieur Elite's home off Boulevard Haussmann that I put my mind to the creeping change over the last one hundred years. You and I are nowhere as rich, on a relative basis, as this guy was, the envy of all, but in almost every other way, we have and do things every day that all the riches in the world back then couldn't buy. Damn, I forgot to mention microwave ovens, or Orville Redenbacher, or . . .

Progress is the simple answer for one hundred years of forward momentum. But that doesn't explain how it happened.

Somewhere along the way, you were probably force-fed some economics. An economy is about commerce and trade and me buying bread from the baker who buys meat from the butcher who buys candlesticks, blah, blah, blah. Econ 101 and all the macro mumbo jumbo of "price is where supply meets demand" and marginal costs meeting marginal utility doesn't explain why I can find cheap flights on Southwest Airlines to Salt Lake City to go skiing, or why I can even afford to go skiing in the first place. Something creates all that wealth that the richest in the world never had, including Kevlar parabolic skis.

How about this line: Economics is about allocating scarce resources. Well, I guess that could work, but that implies there are only so many resources to go around, and that those who pay the most get the scarcest ones. But where did the jet come from, or the Kevlar, or the online travel agent? That definition is unsatisfying.

There is only one definition of an economy I've ever been comfortable with: a system that increases the standard of living of its participants. Period. Everything else from credit to money supply to quarterly earnings releases to minimum wages is just a tool or else a meaningless characteristic of an economy. Without that "increasing living standards" thing, you and I would still be living in caves, chasing squirrels and shoveling shit and dying young from minor infections.

Increasing standards of living doesn't happen automatically. It's not a gift from heaven. Someone has to invent the future.

But how?

How do you find the next big thing? How do you find things that go up and to the right and keep going up and up and up? How do you find companies to work for or to invest in that will let you create some real wealth? And how do you do well by the world?

Thirty years ago, as I started my so-called career, not a single person told me that computers and technology would get so cheap that they would practically end up being given away in boxes of Cheerios. Or that Wall Street and banking and money management would be turned inside out, uncorking money buried inside the musty trust departments of sclerotic banks. Instead of gathering dust, this money went fleeing to the higher returns from money market and mutual funds, thus allowing anyone with an idea to either invest or get access to capital to build a company of their own, go public, and create enormous wealth.

Just one little mention at a cocktail party, from someone, anyone, telling me about this, would have done me wonders. Not a peep!

On top of that, no one told me that tons and tons of jobs would be destroyed—and even more created. Who knew? Yet that's the world I had to navigate.

Today, the economy may have blown up, but the underlying principles of wealth creation still exist. Maybe even stronger than ever. How to tap them is not so obvious. But it's never obvious. You have to figure out how to create the future yourself.

The only way to truly succeed over time is to use your head, think out long-term trends, figure out where productivity exists (and therefore wealth is being created) in the economy, and invest your mind or your money alongside it.

Circus and Inspiration

"IT'S BEEN TOUGH, BUT I'M PRETTY CONFIDENT THAT WE'LL be taken care of."

"Uh-huh."

"We take care of the planet and it will take care of us."

"Uh, I guess."

I'm sitting watching the Golden State Warriors against the Detroit Pistons, but I keep getting distracted by this loud guy behind me babbling away about anything and everything.

"It's a new era. You know what I mean."

"Yeah, uh-huh."

It's early in the game, so the Oracle Arena is pretty quiet. You can hear sneakers squeaking and screeching on the waxed court. And I'm sure half the people in the arena can hear the loudmouth behind me pontificating away.

"Not quite Aquarius, but we're getting there," he continued.

"No more torturing animals. Free doctors. Trains that go everywhere. The sun will feed us and free us."

I can't take it anymore and start to stretch so I can turn around and take a look at this guy. He was straight out of Hollywood casting. Shoulder-length hair parted down the middle, a tie-dyed T-shirt, granny glasses, two earrings, and a distribution of facial hair I have since learned is known as an "imperial." Oh yeah, and it was dyed orange. Hey, buddy, the sixties called. They want their look back.

"We're just using too much stuff," he declared, sipping soda out of a plastic cup. "Everyone is. That's why I'm a no-growther." Oh no. Here it comes. "Put limits on everything. We gotta stop consuming, man, we're killing the planet. And they're not making any more of it."

He was talking to a middle-aged African American couple, both nodding tentatively—they just wanted to watch the game.

"I know all this because I'm in the newspaper business. . . ."

I spit up my beer.

"Oh wow, whereabouts?" the wife asked.

"Just outside of Sonoma."

"Pretty up th . . ."

"Yeah, we're getting killed by corporatism. Plus this thing is hurting us bad." I craned my neck to sneak a peek at him waving an iPhone in front of the darting eyes of the couple. "Local paper. Real old school. My dad and I run it. He started it forty-seven years ago."

"Nice."

"Yeah, it is nice. People need us. We give back, you know?"

"I guess."

"So we've filed for state assistance, there are some historic preservation statutes we're looking into."

"Isn't that for houses?"

"And what do you do?" he asked.

"Lawyer."

"Oh wow. That's great. Good for you. Civil rights?"

"What? Uh, no. Corporate."

"Oh. Cool. I guess. Where?"

"San Ramon." Pause. "I'm with Chevron."

I then hear a dejected, "Oh."

"Oh good, or oh bad?"

"Definitely bad. Sorry, dude. Chevron is the one killing our planet. Noxious carboné, man." Pronounced *Car-Bone-A*. "I'm for exclusive solar and wind. That's it."

"Uh-huh." It didn't sound like a friendly uh-huh.

That didn't stop tie-dye: "We've got to organize, prioritize, and then homogenize."

Whatever that means.

I happen to know that the Detroit Pistons had flown in on a private charter, eating Chevron jet fuel at fifty gallons a minute; I didn't hear orange-fungus-face complaining about that. And the taxpayer-subsidized BART train doesn't quite reach up to Sonoma, so he probably drove himself to the game.

My blood pressure rose. I couldn't see the basketball court anymore, from the red streaks in my eyes blocking my vision. Fortunately, I had the ultimate relief valve for the steam building up and threatening to hiss out of my ears. I called my old college friend Shelby, who lives in Burlington, Vermont, and has built up an immunity to this sort of thing.

"Shelby?"

"Yeah. . . . what time is it?"

"Second quarter."

"What?"

"You sleeping?"

"I was."

"It's kind of an emergency."

"Boho encounter?"

"Stage Three."

"Go on."

I explained what I'd heard so far, and then I let fly, not caring whether he could hear me.

"So here's this boho, never-wanna-grow-up, Peter Pan pinhead guy, milking Daddy's dying school-menu-listing flyer that he probably drives around and throws unwanted onto driveways all over a town that wouldn't exist if it weren't for farm subsidies, lecturing a trained lawyer probably working twelve-hour days and earning well into the 50 percent federal and state and FICA and Medicare marginal tax bracket, who is probably just trying to get by and enjoy a nice basketball game on a Friday night, about what is right and wrong with the economy, humanity, and the world. Isn't that precious?"

"That's only Stage Two."

"Why's that?"

"This guy is an idiot."

"Yeah?"

"And not even unique," Shelby explained, "to this generation or even this era. These types have always been around. Poseurs, beats, Canadians. There are just more of them lately because we've been on such a rocket ride of prosperity over the past twenty or thirty years. Prosperity breeds lethargy, complacency, stagnation, false expectations, a sense of entitlement, and a lack of creativity."

"Yeah, but—"

"Capital and creativity are inversely related," Shelby interrupted. "You know that."

"I just live on the innovation side of things, and this guy . . ."

"Yeah, yeah." Shelby seemed to be shaking off sleep and gathering his thoughts. "Look, there has been lots of innovation over the past few decades. But think about how much more would have been possible if assholes like him were innovating too. If we could have engaged even ten percent more of our collective resources. This boho, hell, some huge chunk of the general population is entertaining itself in the trivial, self-absorbed activity of watching meaningless competition that squanders huge amounts of resources." I think he's talking about the NBA game, and I'm guilty as charged. "And he's got the gall to spout off about wind power and the evil of corporate lawyers who probably wouldn't be necessary if morons like him didn't bite the hand that feeds them by suing snail darters. Message to our kids: get back to basics. Develop and deploy the skills to hunt and gather for yourself and your tribe, but with today's technologies. And tell them to stop wasting their time watching a bunch of freakishly tall folks run around in Chuck Taylors and start doing something useful. Beer and professional sports are today's bread and circuses that Caesar used to sedate the masses. Right now, we have no time for trivia."

"You done?"

"Hell no."

"You sound angry. Don't get mad, get even. Punch the brownies. Isn't that what you taught me?" I asked. Shelby once smashed an entire counter of brownies at a deli when the boho behind the counter insisted that all sandwiches had to have alfalfa sprouts.

"Maybe. I gotta get some sleep." It was close to midnight on the East Coast.

"Yeah, see ya. And thanks."

But Shelby is right. This is what we've come to, isn't it? Claims of moral authority from someone who hasn't contributed a single thing to society. Nothing. This guy is a leech, a mooch, yet he's the first to nod in smug self-satisfaction to any of the false choices for "improving" the world, from "outlawing fossil fuels" to "using less stuff."

But I've learned not to get mad. Not anymore.

Getting even means outperforming the mooches.

Come to think of it, it wouldn't be a fair fight. Yes, if you want to make the world better it will take you lots of hard work swimming upstream against rapids and rocks and the unknown, but you'll be in an ever-smaller cadre of those doing the inventing. The rest of the world, despite their whining, will line up around the block to pay up for what you invent because it will make their lives just a little bit better. Some very smart people developed and manufactured the iPhone, and this guy paid them for it even as he cursed them for destroying his industry.

We have a moral imperative to do well, to invent the future, to create wealth, to raise everyone else's standard of living, if only to make up for those like Imperial who are an anchor on progress.

I HAVE TO ADMIT, part of the inspiration for this book is Saul Alinsky's book *Rules for Radicals*. Written in 1971, the book gained attention once more during the 2008 presidential campaign. The year 1971 was part of an era of violent protest, Weather Underground bombings, campus protests, riots, and of course Walter Cronkite telling us, "That's the way it is," as though there were nothing anyone could do about it.

Alinsky, sometimes referred to as the "legendary amoral guru of left-wing activism," was an influence on Barack Obama in his early political days. Michelle Obama quoted from the book at the Democratic National Convention the night before her husband was nominated as the party's presidential candidate, talking about "the world as it is" and "the world as it should be." Hey, it seemed to work. I wondered what I was missing. I find most politics entertaining theater, but not knowing much about community organizing, I ponied up $10.94 for the book with free two-day shipping from Amazon, and dug right in.

Hoping to be enlightened, I was amused and then inspired. Not to be a community organizer, mind you; I suspect the world has plenty of those. But it got me wondering. Maybe I could figure out how those inventions (that the dead rich French dude never had) came about, and how to create the next set of world-changing things.

By the way, Alinsky didn't have a clue. He just wanted to steal your stuff and give it to his friends. Really. The book itself is dull and repetitive and a bit insulting. It implies that we are all easily manipulated, which is probably true, but still annoying. Its fault is that it paints a static world. The pie is fixed and we are fighting over the size of the slices. You have it, we want it, let's take it from you. "That's the way it is."

In describing his rules and goals, Alinsky continually argues against yelling at representatives in government to effect change. Instead, one should become the representative in government and effect the change one wants. Alinsky's formula is simple: Turn against the establishment, organize the community, lie if you have to, get elected, and then become the establishment. Once in office, use government as you desire to help/pay back/redistribute to those who got you into power.

Holman Jenkins summarized it best in a *Wall Street Journal* column on the auto industry: "The doyen of community organizing, [Alinsky and his] views profoundly influenced Mr. Obama. The late Alinsky was unsentimental about power, and about accumulating it in order to extract from 'the system' benefits for his constituents."

The book goes on and on about Haves and Have-nots. Alinsky writes, "On top are the Haves, with power, money, food, security, and luxury. They suffocate in their surpluses while the Have-Nots starve . . . Thermopolitically, they are cold and determined to freeze the status quo." Never mind how the Haves actually generated their power and money; that's irrelevant, at least to Alinsky. More on this later.

He goes on, "On the bottom are the world's Have-Nots . . . Caged by color, physical or political, they are barred from an opportunity to represent themselves in the politics of life. The Haves want to keep; the Have-Nots want to get . . . They hate the establishment of the Haves with its arrogant opulence, its police, its courts, and its churches." And in between, Alinsky characterizes the Have-a-Little, Want-Mores, the middle class, who are filled with Do-Nothings who "function as blankets whenever possible smothering sparks of dissension that promise to flare up into the fire of action." Great poetry, but maybe the middle class is just scrambling to get ahead and become Haves themselves rather than looking for a handout.

In other words, big business and the establishment, whatever that even means anymore, are bad. The impoverished are the good guys, just trying to get their due. Which is okay, claims Alinsky, no matter their tactics. There is an entire chapter, "Of Means and Ends," with a lovely call to action, in italics no less, claiming "the means-and-ends moralists or non-doers always end up on their ends without any means." Alinsky provides the license to do whatever it takes.

Alinsky's harshest critics claim his goal was radical socialism and redistribution of wealth. Maybe that's true, maybe not. But the guy is dead, well before I could ask him one simple question, which is how was all that wealth you planned on giving away created in the first place? To redistribute it, someone has to create it. Lots and lots of wealth has been created since 1971 and I don't think it was stolen from the Incas. Even gold in your backyard is worthless without the hard work and ingenuity involved in digging it up.

So how? Governments don't create wealth. They are almost always behind the ball. Policy tends to follow, not lead, economics. Things that better our lives are created and then government steps in with a set of laws to govern their use. Radio technology is invented which leads to the creation of a Federal Communications Commission to allocate scarce radio frequencies, which they still haven't gotten right. Lifesaving drugs are invented and the Food and Drug Administration regulates how they can be administered.

Don't get me wrong. Government can certainly create an environment where commerce can live, where capital and labor can combine and create productive things. Free people, strong property rights, and transparent markets often do the trick, and rules and regulations to enable these can set inventors loose to do great things. But too many rules and regulations slow down change, stifle innovation, maintain the status quo. Because of the Post Office monopoly on first- and third-class mail, we still lick stamps and slap them on envelopes in an era of instantly delivered electronic mail.

At the end of the day, this is Alinsky's complaint. The status quo is oppressive. Down with the establishment. You're living in poverty, so it must be someone else's fault, most likely those big ugly corporations that are stealing us blind. He provides some rules (of questionable morals) to effect change, such as:

Rule 1: "Power is not only what you have, but what the enemy thinks you have."

Rule 12: "Pick the target, freeze it, personalize it, and polarize it. Cut off the support network and isolate the target from sympathy. Go after people and not institutions; people hurt faster than institutions. (This is cruel, but very effective. Direct, personalized criticism and ridicule works.)"

But Alinsky's change is about the redistribution of wealth, not the creation of wealth. Move it from one pile to another. *Viva La Revolución.* Smart in an era of landowners and peasants, I suppose, but not in a productivity-driven economy, where the output of the human mind creates wealth, not just spreading a bunch of manure around to grow crops (or write a book).

Alinsky wasn't writing about the 1970s—he was writing about the 1790s!

Ask Lenin: You can take over government, but you can't create wealth. Certain people can get rich, yes, but only as long as others are creating wealth for them to steal. Creating societal wealth? Dream on.

The funny thing is that, at the same time Alinsky was writing his book, Intel engineers Federico Faggin and Ted Hoff were designing tiny circuits so a Japanese calculator company, Busicom, could sell a cheap calculator, the Nippon Calculator. How very establishment-ish, no? They made Intel's very first microprocessor, the 4004, programmable, because it was easier than doing a custom design; plus, the Japanese weren't 100 percent sure what functions they actually wanted. And when Busicom went belly up,

Intel could sell the 4004 to other companies for their own custom calculators.

This single programmable device, with constant upgrading through today's Core processors in a never-ending march of progress, did more to augment human brains, create jobs (by destroying others), increase productivity, create wealth, bolster the U.S. economy, destroy communism, and provide aid to the rest of the world than any bunch of community organizers getting elected, raising taxes, and fixing toilets in subsidized housing. It was *plus c'est la même chose, plus ça change.* Despite five years of French, I'm sure I've still butchered it, but what I'm trying to say is the more things stayed the same, the more they changed. The more the status quo prevailed, the easier it was for someone to undercut it, take it out at the knees and change things for the better. Inventing a new future not, I should note, by redistributing the past, but by destroying it.

After the 2008 Wall Street meltdown, we are clearly in an era of bigger government. But unless you outlaw science and research, you can't keep good technology down. It's going to be invented. While some are focused on redistributing wealth, others (hint, hint) will be creating it.

When I finished Alinsky's book, I stopped laughing and got angry. My first thought was that Alinsky can kiss my ass. Alinsky can keep his Haves and his Have-nots. It's really more about the Makes and the Takes, isn't it? It's not zero sum. Someone's Making wealth, while others are Taking it.

Redistributing wealth helps a swath of society, but progress comes from creating wealth in the first place. Don't Take it, Make it!

We don't need any more redistributionist radicals like Saul Alinsky; we need Free Radicals.

Wait a second. Free Radical. Free Radical. That has a certain ring to it. I like how that sounds. I think I'll use it.

A free radical, if I remember my tenth-grade chemistry, is an atom or molecule with unpaired electrons. Because they have a free electron, these free radicals are highly reactive; they are always looking for something to do, hungry for some chemical reaction— like combustion.

So what then is a Free Radical? I've read about them throughout history, run across them, worked with them, invested in them, and seen them all my life. But not until now have I really thought about how to classify this type of person.

I guess in its simplest form, a Free Radical is someone who not only creates wealth for themselves, but at the very same time, improves the world, makes life better, and increases everyone else's standard of living.

Charles Curtis's 1903 steam turbine generator brought electricity to the masses. Using that electricity, in 1907, James Spangler, a janitor with asthma, invented an electric suction-sweeper, today's vacuum cleaner. William David Coolidge's thermionic X-ray tube of 1913 changed medicine. That same year, the Walker brothers in Philadelphia invented the first electric dishwasher. In 1916, Clarence Birdseye perfected the flash-freezing process (and Birds Eye potato puffs). In 1928, Thomas Midgley, Albert Henne, and Robert McNary synthesized the first chlorofluorocarbons (trademarked as Freon in 1930), ushering in safe refrigerators and air conditioning (other coolants eventually replaced Freon). Paul M. Zoll created the cardiac pacemaker in 1952. And Percy L. Spencer in 1945 watched a magnetron melt candy, leading to the invention of microwave ovens.

Lots of housecleaners lost their jobs to vacuum cleaners. Lots of servants weren't hired or husbands yelled at because of electric dishwashers. Freezers and Birds Eye frozen food put a lot of cooks out of work and on and on.

Free Radicals found situations to combust and destroy, but in the end, it was only to make room to build the new—disrupt the status quo, do more with less, advance society, drive progress rather than have progress drive them.

A Free Radical is someone who gets wealthy inventing the future by helping others live longer and better. Rather than be a burden on society or tax society or milk society for all it's worth, a Free Radical improves society and is paid handsomely for doing so.

Rather than building huts in Costa Rica, a Free Radical invents cheaper building materials, improves the logistics of getting materials where they need to be, creates a market to discover the right prices for materials and labor, educates Costa Ricans, hires them to do twenty-first-century work well beyond the grueling labor in sweatshops of the Far East—and in the end, they can afford to build their own homes. A Free Radical doesn't even have to set foot in Costa Rica to be a hero, though likely an unsung one.

Create wealth and change the world. It sounds oxymoronic. Do good by doing well. It sounds like a rationalization for someone getting rich, but you've seen it just like I have. Ted Hoff invented the microprocessor and has changed billions of lives for the better. Lloyd Conover invented the antibiotic tetracycline and has probably saved a billion lives from early demise. Larry Page and Sergey Brin perfected search and created wealth not only for themselves but for everyone who plugs into their electronic ecosystem.

Free Radicals, all of them. It's not the only way to get wealthy, but it's the most rewarding for the rest of us.

You can be a Free Radical, too.

■   ■   ■

BUT HOW? AS I mentioned, I've been around and analyzed Free Radicals all my life—the Gordon Moores, the Mark Cubans, the Steve Jobses, but I've never thought all that much about what it takes to become one. So with that in mind, I started surfing around to see if anyone else had thought this through. One afternoon, searching for some hints at how to find the elusive wealth and progress combo, I tripped across something called the 99% Conference, a New York powwow of hundreds of "creative thinkers" (who could obviously afford the $490 admission) to discuss issues like productivity and execution, turning ideas into reality. Man, I thought to myself, I've gotta be close. My fingers started twitching on my mouse. Their Web site practically screamed at me: "It's not about ideas. It's about making ideas happen."

After that setup, I'm sorry I missed the conference. No matter. Luckily, Nicole Wong, a journalist and blogger for the Web site VentureBeat, was there, and summarized the themes that emerged from two days of talks and panels and chitchat in the hallways, thus saving me (and you) almost five hundred hard-earned dollars:

1. Engage in personal projects and things that you love.

2. Share your ideas and listen to other people's.

3. Prioritize your projects so you don't sabotage yourself by trying to do everything.

4. Do what makes sense.

5. Be proactive.

Really? That's it? What kind of load of crap is that? I might have to call Shelby again to calm me down. I was hoping for so much more. This might as well have come from some inspirational speaker, Tony Robbins for techies or something. This list provides no order from chaos, just platitudes that might as well have been found inside fortune cookies.

I kept searching . . . and searching . . . and searching. But no one's done it. Yeah, sure, there are plenty of guides to get rich. For a mere $25, Suze Orman or David Bach or Dave Ramsey will surely tell you how to get rich and stay rich. Good luck with that. Tim Ferriss says you only have to work four hours a week. Sign me up! I've met Tim and like him—everyone does. He's a bouncy fellow who thinks a million miles a minute—and I'll bet he works 24/7. Phil Town says it only takes fifteen minutes a week to get rich. And speaking of lots of brain cycles, even my friend Jim Cramer will tell you how to stay mad and harness the stock market for personal gain.

I've never wanted to write a guidebook; it goes against my personal code. I've never wanted to go on the road and teach investors the inside tricks of the trade. Never wanted to be an investment guru or life coach or anything that reeks of "positive adult development." Yuck. But, I realized, no one has ever put down on paper how to get rich the right way, by helping society get rich as well. No one ever wrote a set of rules to find things with enormous upside and enormous potential to change the world. How to find, create, leverage, and ride the Next Big Thing.

So I broke my own rule, took matters into my own hands, and wrote my own set of Rules for Free Radicals. Inspired by the 99%ers (kinda) and by Saul Alinsky (sorta), I dug deep into my time in Silicon Valley, on Wall Street, working with smart people, watching what works and what doesn't, and thinking long and hard as to why, and I came up with a master list of 12 Rules (plus a baker's dozen bonus rule).

I'll sum up the book you're about to read as follows: You should be a scalable, wasteful, horizontal, edge-hugging, Tom Sawyer-ish, productive, human-adapting, people-eating, market-driven, exceptional, market-entrepreneuring, zero-marginal, virtual-pipe-controlling return maximizer.

Let me see if I can explain.

If It Doesn't Scale, It Will Get Stale

Let's START WITH THE BASICS.

I figured out long ago that the things in my world that become huge successes (computer chips, cell phones, network equipment) always have the same characteristic—they get cheaper every year. And every time they get cheaper, some new application pops up to take advantage of them at their new, lower cost. As costs go down, demand rises. Economists call this elasticity. Techies call it Learning Curves. They all mean the same thing—*Scale*.

In 1968, Intel introduced the 3101, a 64-bit memory chip. The original price was $40. Or about a buck a bit. Hardly anyone cared. At the time, almost all computer memories in IBM and everyone else's mainframes were core memories, a ferromagnetic ceramic material with a wire wrapped around it that could be magnetized in two directions, representing the binary 1 for on, and 0 for off. These were often assembled by hand.

Still, a few people bought Intel's chip. The 3101 was a bit finicky, hard to use in a real computer, and only held 64 bits. It was a novelty. But the funny thing was, at a dollar a bit, it was competitive with core memories. Still, no one really cared.

The 1101 256-bit memory came out in 1969, again mostly to yawns. Some computer designers used it for shift registers inside the brains of the mainframe, but it didn't displace core memory.

In 1972, the 1103 1-kilobit dynamic RAM hit the market. For the same $40, more or less, you got 1,024 bits of storage. Now you were paying about 4 cents a bit. The 1103 became the best-selling semiconductor part that year, and kept on going. It started displacing core memory, although rather slowly. Up until 1976, 95 percent of memory sold was core memory. But these dynamic RAM semiconductor chips made inroads. The mainframe guys like IBM were slow to catch on, but the minicomputer companies like Digital Equipment, Data General, and Wang started using these solid state memory chips so they could sell their computers cheaply, undercutting mainframes and growing their market. Every time the price point per bit dropped, they would buy more of them.

I figured this all out early in my life as an analyst on Wall Street, and milked it for over twenty years. Elastic demand, new applications, growing market. Woohoo!

Today, my iPhone has 16 gigabytes, or 128 gigabits (a byte is 8 bits), of memory, for around $500 without the contract. Now, not all of the cost is for the memory, but if it were, that would be about 4 billionths of a cent for a bit, or a billion-fold decline over forty years.

Another way to look at it is that in 1972, an iPhone at a buck a bit would cost $128 billion, if you could even build it in the first place. Maybe you could sell one to the Pentagon. But who would bother writing applications for it? Instead, it's under $500 and more than 70 million have been sold so far, and eventually smartphones will be a $128 or maybe $256 billion market, with a billion sold, instead of just one.

Now that, in a nutshell, is scale. Pure and simple. You lower something's cost and make it more abundant, again and again and again. You sell millions and billions of it. And everyone who buys one has an economic rationalization—it makes them more productive. You can listen to music with earphones instead of hiring the New York Philharmonic (or AC/DC) to perform live in your kitchen. Or send an e-mail instead of tying a message to a pigeon's leg. Or click "I'm Feeling Lucky," instead of pestering librarians to look up the life story of Cornelius Vanderbilt. You get the point.

Several trillion dollars of wealth have been created from the Scaling of bits. You can look at the market capitalization of all the tech companies, from Intel to Microsoft to Google to whoever else, and you get a trillion. The other trillion or so is the lower costs that companies like Wal-Mart and Morgan Stanley and Merck have been able to enjoy because computing power gets cheaper each and every year.

One-off cost decline is not Scale. Cost decline that goes on for a decade or several decades is Scale, something that you can build an entire economy on.

Free Radicals find things that Scale year in and year out.

The other way to think about Scale is in terms of numbers. Is the market for what you're doing a thousand people? Ten thousand? That's okay, but not Scale-worthy.

A Free Radical should ask—can it be used by a million people? Ten million? A billion? Now that's something that Scales. This is the question I ask every time I look at a new product, a start-up, or a new industry. I instantly lose my baked-in biases of what something costs today, or what it can do today for a given cost of, say, $500, and just mentally slide down the cost curve.

Of course, to get to a billion people, it has to get cheaper. Not overnight, but over time, over decades perhaps. But understand that what you are doing can continue marching down that cost curve and Scale to millions and billions.

Not sure? Be damn sure.

AFTER I GRADUATED from college as an electrical engineer, I got a job at Bell Labs, the research arm of AT&T. At the time, Ma Bell required a master's degree to work in the Labs. Back then, AT&T was a regulated monopoly with so much money flowing in that they probably had it stuffed in burlap sacks. For a long time, you could only lease your phone from AT&T, not buy it. Anyway, they (or rather, you the American taxpayer!) sent me to grad school, "One Year On Campus," I think they called it. They paid for school and gave me a stipend of a thousand dollars a month. Beer money and then some.

They killed that program a year later and the monopoly busted; AT&T was split into Baby Bells in 1983. But it was still a fun place to work. I spent about five years there and no one ever told me what to do. I designed chips, wrote code, got to spend a million or so bucks a year on completely unnecessary computers and other stuff. Even better, I left at eleven for long lunches and came back after two. Saying "late lunch" always worked.

My group had designed the famous Bell 212A 1200-baud modem—it transmitted 1200 bits per second. AT&T was in no hurry to upgrade it to a faster speed until the day a judge decided that everything developed with regulated dollars should be available and licensable to all takers. Companies like Hayes and US-Robotics would license AT&T's designs and get into business, usually undercutting AT&T's prices. This would eventually light a fire under AT&T. (In other words, competition works. But that's old news.)

Others got to 2400 baud, then 4800 baud way before us; after all, no need to rush inside a big company. One day, bored and probably slightly beer-goggled after a late lunch, I perused an org chart with my name, my boss's, the director's, the executive director's, and finally a vice president's name, a guy who had maybe a couple of thousand people who reported up to him. Then, just for fun, I took out another org chart, one that had everyone from the top down—Chairman Charles Brown, the CEO, the CFO, presidents of various divisions and executive vice presidents, first vice presidents, double secret vice presidents. Command and control companies love org charts! It was a huge sea of mostly old men's faces. But what struck me the most was the disconnect between the top of my org chart and the bottom of the corporate chart. There was a band gap, a void, a black hole, for goodness sake. I was at least fifteen layers down from the top, but because of the disconnect, it might be more like twenty or more layers of management. I got the hell out of there by the end of the year.

I was twenty-five years old when I cashed out my forced savings plan, the only money I had in the world: a whopping $324. Hey, I was in my early twenties and spent all my salary on fun and frivolity. That $324 wasn't going to go far, so I started the world's smallest company, me, and taught programming and chip design courses. I tried to get consulting jobs but floundered; who on Earth would consult with a twenty-five-year-old about anything?

And yet, I had the inklings of an idea about all these ever-cheaper chips being made in Silicon Valley, that all these computers connected with phone lines could turn into this giant, well, something. I wasn't really sure. I was in the fog, but could barely make out something interesting. I didn't think up the Internet; Al Gore did that much later. Actually, the Internet, in a crude form, already existed. All I did was imagine a world of cheap computers and connected computers that I had seen in a vastly more expensive form at Bell Labs. This informed my investment decisions for the rest of my life. Didn't know what I was on to at the time, of course.

Luckily, I tripped across an opening for an investment analyst at Paine Webber. I wasn't familiar with Wall Street or even Paine Webber, beyond Jimmy Connors's "Thank you, Paine Webber" commercials. I wondered if they made tennis grips or something. But the investment bank hired me, taking a chance that an engineer might do a better job than an economist or an MBA at analyzing all these rapidly growing chip companies like Intel and Motorola and Texas Instruments.

A bull market had just started on Wall Street, which was going through enormous changes of its own. There had been a tech IPO boom the year before and no one had any idea which of these companies were worth investing in, or if it was even a growth business. Of course, I had no clue either. But I jumped in, studied the dynamics of the business, and figured out that every year, no matter what, 30 percent comes out of the cost of each transistor in these chips, every gate, every function gets smaller, cheaper, faster. This was the economic version of Gordon Moore's observation that chip density doubles every eighteen months—Moore's law. But while costs halved, the number of bits sold more than doubled. I looked under the covers and figured out there was a weird economic model to all of this. It was an elastic business. Every time you lowered the cost per bit, some new application opened up to take advantage of the cheaper functionality. If you halve prices and sales more than double, you've got a growth business. That's elasticity. Scale.

Chips would get cheaper, and some company would design them into a new product—such as using memory in laser printers to store the image of the page before printing it—and before long the new product would get cheaper and they would sell zillions of them. So all I had to do was watch for the price of some chip to drop. Wall Street hates when prices drop. If the price of Kraft singles drops, the stock goes down. But in tech, it is what creates the growth. So Intel would announce a price drop and everyone would hate technology stocks (because, again, Wall Street loves companies that raise prices, believing that rising prices are the only path to higher profits). Stock prices would inevitably drop, and then I'd close my eyes, count to ten, and the whole thing would take off in a bigger way than even I had imagined, stocks going up by five or ten times—a feeding frenzy. Something gets cheaper and you sell more of it, more than making up for the price drop. The opposite of cigarettes. And of course the Learning Curve works in your favor. Make one or two of something and it's expensive. Make a million and it gets so cheap that everyone starts using it—you end up selling tens or hundreds of millions.

I squinted hard enough and could make out that laser printers were going to drop from $10,000 to under $1,000. What I didn't figure was that within a few years, and coupled with some Adobe Photoshop and Aldus PageMaker software, every aspiring publisher would start a magazine and lay out the pages themselves. Instead of expensive type shops, it happened on a screen. But sure enough, the magazine business boomed and the PC and laser printer and software and everything else that touched it boomed and a trillion in wealth was created out of thin air, or out of thin silicon anyway. What did I know about magazines? You only had to know about Scale, not how it was going to be used.

Modems Scaled too. They hit 9600 baud, 14.4 and 28.8 and then 56 kilobit, before traditional modems hit a wall and were replaced by 200-kilobit DSL that worked over phone lines, followed by 1-megabit cable modems that became the 5-megabit broadband cable modems of today. (By the way, today's modems could run at 100 megabits if it weren't for the monopolists that own the cable lines holding us back. More on that later.)

THERE ARE TONS of examples of Free Radicals in action, driving costs lower and leveraging Scale. I've found quite a few. You might not label them as Free Radicals, but they were, because they constantly drove down costs.

On August 27, 1859, next to a trickle of running water in western Pennsylvania, Edwin Drake struck oil. The well, known as McClintock No. 1, spit out tons of oil, and before long pipelines were laid to run it to trains and ships. John D. Rockefeller built the colossal and feared (monopolies are always feared!) Standard Oil. Teddy Roosevelt rode to the rescue, on horseback no doubt, and busted the trust in 1911. I learned all this in eighth-grade history—less discussed is the economics of the whole thing.

Lighting was none too cheap before the Civil War. Candles and whale oil (*Moby-Dick* was published in 1851) were luxury items. The rich could read at night—and the rest sat around in the dark and probably drank moonshine. But by 1865, the price of forty-two gallons of petrochemical oil, barrel included, cost around twenty-five dollars. Seven years later, in 1872, because of Rockefeller's help in creating increased supply and much better distribution, the price of that filled barrel was under ten dollars. Less than two decades after that the cost had dropped to $3.36.

Whales around the world rejoiced.

The cost to read at night with kerosene lights dropped to a penny an hour, opening up the market for lighting (and books) to the world's middle class. The market for kerosene exploded (though not literally).

We can argue whether Rockefeller's Standard Oil had excess profits and needed to be broken up, but the reality is the oil market was extremely elastic, to the betterment of society. And oil producers, Rockefeller included, by pricing just above their ever-lower costs in a rapidly growing market, made a fortune. So Rockefeller was a Free Radical, at least for a while. He increased the supply of oil, got it delivered to the market, and enabled cheap lighting for huge swaths of society, increasing their standard of living. At some point Rockefeller stopped being a Free Radical and instead became a ruthless businessman, or more likely criminal, blowing up his competitors' oil pipelines so he could control distribution. But you can't take away the benefit of ever-cheaper light and heat that he and others brought to millions.

HERE'S ANOTHER ONE. After the Civil War, demand for railroads boomed. The Golden Spike creating the first transcontinental railroad was hammered at Promontory Summit, Utah, in 1869 by Leland Stanford. But the pricing and economic part of this story are rarely discussed, which is why history teachers usually don't teach math.

The rails, obviously, are the key component of any railroad. Originally, metallurgists melted iron ore by mixing it with burning wood (charcoal), and then poured it into a mold to get cast iron. Cast iron has a high carbon content, 3 to 5 percent, which makes it hard but brittle. Not a great choice for rails. So the railroad companies needed a way to get the carbon and other impurities out of the iron. Puddling furnaces were invented to melt the iron in a vat, separate from the charcoal fire. A puddler opened and closed an opening between the iron and the charcoal to keep the heat just right as well as to oxidize the carbon out of the molten iron. Chunks of solid iron would appear, be gathered together, hammered somewhat flat, and then run through rollers into flat sheets which could be cut into rails. Phew.

This wrought iron had very low carbon content, less than a tenth of 1 percent, which made it hard but malleable enough to bend into curves for railroads. Most antebellum railroads were made out of this wrought iron; it served, but heavily trafficked stretches needed to be replaced every couple of months. What was needed was something with maybe one or one and a half percent carbon, hard enough to last a long time and malleable enough to be practical. In other words, steel.

In 1856, British scientist and future Free Radical Henry Bessemer invented a process similar to the puddling furnace, but one which involved blasting compressed air into the molten iron via holes in the bottom. In a matter of minutes, carbon and silicon were oxidized out. But we want more carbon, not less. The damn thing worked too well, so another Brit named Robert Mushet invented a material containing manganese, carbon, and iron that got added to the vat. The manganese combined with the oxygen, leaving behind exactly as much carbon as desired. Voilà, high-quality steel with just the right amount of carbon from a cheap, controlled (and highly patented, with over a hundred of them) process. They didn't invent steel, they just invented a high-volume process to manufacture it cheaply. Just what was needed to spit out rails.

Soon, competitors were attempting other ways to make cheaper steel. For instance, German engineer Karl Wilhelm Siemens, another future Free Radical, created a process that uses gas to heat the furnace and added iron to dilute the initially high carbon content. Nothing like engineers to do the exact opposite of what already works to improve things.

Okay, now here's the fun part.

According to Professor Joseph S. Spoerl at Saint Anselm College, "in 1867, 460,000 tons of wrought iron rails were made and sold for $83 per ton; only 2550 tons of Bessemer steel rails were made, fetching a price of up to $170 per ton."

So even eleven years after Bessemer invented his steel process, it cost twice as much and had less than 1 percent of the market. Makes sense.

But, "by 1884, iron rails had virtually ceased to be made at all; steel rails had replaced them at an annual production of 1,500,000 tons selling at a price of $32 per ton."

Now that's elasticity. Prices drop 60 percent and production more than triples. And hidden in the raw numbers is the fact that the steel rails lasted a decade or more and allowed for railroad cars to be loaded up, an increase in weight from "eight tons to seventy."

The businessman Andrew Carnegie jumped all over the Bessemer process, putting up capital and building steel mills to pump out rails for railroads and pipes for oil pipelines, eventually merging his company with Henry Clay Frick's coal and coke mining company to form U.S. Steel to meet the spike in demand. By the end of the nineteenth century, Carnegie got the price of steel down to $14 per ton, a twelfth of the cost three decades prior.

Yeah, yeah, Carnegie and Frick also led one of the nastiest labor lockouts during the Homestead Strike in 1892. At some point they became monopolists and stopped being Free Radicals. The ends don't justify the means, but you can't overlook the gains in everyone's living standards from the elasticity of ever-lower steel prices.

Later, Carnegie sought to regain his good name by donating much of his fortune to building some 2,500 libraries across the United States. Today, he is known as both a nasty businessman and a philanthropist. But if you study his life carefully, you might notice that his work as a Free Radical, lowering the cost of steel by 92 percent in thirty-three years, did more for progress and living standards and affected more people in a positive way than building all those libraries, and yet the good attached to Carnegie's name comes from his charitable work while the bad comes from his business practices. Oh well. History creates its own narratives, but economic history is often much clearer.

WHAT ABOUT FREE Radicals a tad more recent than Rockefeller and Carnegie? Look at Sam Walton. He didn't drive down the price of oil or rails, let alone invent chips or write code. Just modern retail.

After operating a bunch of variety stores as part of the Ben Franklin chain and a Walton's Five and Dime in Bentonville, Arkansas, in 1962, Walton opened Wal-Mart Discount City in Rogers, Arkansas. By 1975, with over a hundred stores and $340 million in sales, Walton leased an IBM mainframe so he could keep track of his inventory as well as figure out if each store was making money or not. No big deal today, but pretty sophisticated for the 1970s. Better inventory control meant he had lower carrying costs, which meant he could cut prices on goods in his store and undercut the competition.

Retail 101. But it meant really tight controls, so Walton put electronic cash registers in stores so he could figure out exactly what was sold. By 1977, he had set up a system to electronically order products directly from suppliers when their inventory was low. By 1979, Wal-Mart topped $1 billion in sales. Lower costs drove market share—what a concept! In 1983, Walton was early in using bar codes to better track sales and inventory, again to drive lower carrying costs. He invested heavily in computers and networks while his competitors stuck to manual techniques and mechanical registers. This is how you get retail to Scale.

In 1987, with close to $10 billion in sales, Wal-Marts around the country were networked with a satellite communications system, and by 1992 the company started using a system called Retail Link so suppliers could automatically replenish shelves, keeping inventory at just the right level. It's classic Intelligence at the Edge (I'll get to that later). By 1995, sales were close to $100 billion.

Sales today are about $400 billion, with some seven thousand stores around the world.

The Walton family are multibillionaires. And rightfully so. They figured out how to use ever-cheaper technology to scale what had previously been seen as an unscaleable, inelastic business. Wal-Mart gets a lot of grief for undercutting local merchants, and for their hiring practices and notorious low pay and health benefits for some two million employees. But by lowering the costs of meat and bread and clothes and books and auto parts and shoes and TVs and just about everything else, Sam Walton improved the lives of more people, by allowing them to afford more and better things, than almost anyone in history. He lowered prices instead of raising them. He got rich by helping everyone else get richer by stretching their income further. A classic Free Radical.

Look, I'm not writing all this so some wealthy folks or their descendants can feel good or shake a bad reputation. I'm just making the point that Scale has created fortunes, for those who created the Scale and for those who benefited from lower prices.

How do you figure out if something will Scale or will end up a dud?

Henry Ford's famous line might help: "Never own anything you have to feed or paint." He meant a horse and a barn. I heard it, I liked it, I use it!

Autos back in Henry Ford's assembly line days replaced expensive horses, but that game ended many decades ago ago. There were no more horses to replace. More progress meant more innovation. On the other hand, designing electronic fuel injection meant you could lower the cost of engines and sell millions of copies of this innovative device, so there is always something that can Scale within a long-dead business. Ford said something else: "If I'd asked my customers what they wanted, they'd have said a faster horse." I suspect Henry Ford figured he could lower the cost of automobiles a lot more easily than the cost of a horse.

Photography Scaled by replacing portrait painting, and then stopped when Kodak raised prices on film every year. Then digital cameras and digital photography got the sector to Scale again, lowering the cost of photos year in, year out, selling more and more cameras until the sensors were cheap enough to include in every cell phone and digital cameras sold in the hundreds of millions. Now face detection and even smile detection—which holds the shot until the whole family is grinning at once—are driving sales.

In medicine, aspirin is a great example of a product that Scaled, though most medicine today goes up in price. Marry biology and electronics and someone will get it to get cheaper every year and Scale. Smells like opportunity.

And on and on.

You CAN WORK in a business that doesn't Scale, one that grows only as fast as the economy, plus or minus a few percentage points. Or you can find a business that Scales and watch it double every year for years and years. Scale makes all the difference.

So how do you recognize Scale? The trick is to find something where the price goes down and the demand goes up. My test is quite simple: I ask myself, if this were cheaper next year, would I buy more? Or would other people buy more? Or will it show up in something new that we all have to have? Does it scale to a million people using it? Or maybe a billion people using it?

Sometimes something that should Scale stops scaling, often because of self-inflicted wounds. eBay's online auctions grew and grew because they let buyers and sellers meet each other cheaply. But for inexplicable reasons, eBay made a habit of raising prices every year instead of lowering them. For a good six or seven years it didn't matter; the company grew and their stock kept going up. But eventually the higher prices caught up with them and now they're just another company looking to acquire businesses like PayPal and Skype for growth.

On the other hand, some things get cheaper but don't Scale. Drugs for irritable bowel syndrome don't scale. Cigarettes don't scale. Twinkies don't scale. Coffee doesn't scale. And I'm not quite sure energy scales anymore.

If a leukemia drug got cheaper every year, I don't think any more doses would be sold. It's inelastic, which is probably why its price won't ever drop.

Don't get me wrong. Some drugs and medical devices have the ability to scale. As medical costs rise, especially surgeries and the cost of many overnight stays at a hospital for recovery, drugs or procedures that postpone or eliminate surgery can save money. Cholesterol-lowering drugs are sold on the premise of eliminating heart attacks (the jury is still out on that). If a $1,000 drug can eliminate a $30,000 surgery, then you have Scale. Colonoscopies find polyps in your colon to nip cancer in the bud, so to speak. But these things only scale if their costs keep dropping, instead of just offering one-off cost savings.

How about lawyers. Do they Scale? Nope. Their price goes up every year with the cost of living—to increase sales, law firms need to hire more lawyers and generate more billable hours. Same for doctors—consultants too. The only way to grow is to add more people or raise prices.

Scale is exactly the opposite. Find some productive task and figure out how you can make it cheaper year by year so you can sell more. Book publishing? Well, it used to Scale, probably for the hundred years after the Gutenberg press was invented when you no longer had to copy books by adding monks writing longhand! And now it is starting to Scale again—electronic books can't happen fast enough.

Google isn't built on cheap servers and cheap bandwidth; it's built on ever-cheaper servers and ever-cheaper bandwidth—on a continuum. It makes a difference. The trick is to find something that Scales over a long period of time to build your productivity on.

The history of wealth creation shows this as well. Find the cost decline, find the Scale, and you will find the wealth.

Waste What's Abundant to Make Up for What's Scarce

ON ONE OF HIS FREQUENT TRIPS TO SILICON VALLEY, I invited my friend George Gilder to dinner. George is always getting labeled as an author and a futurist, which is somewhat redundant as he often writes books about what the future is going to look like. His 1981 book *Wealth and Poverty* pretty much laid out the next twenty-five years as they happened, but then he fell in love with technology, writing *Microcosm* and *Telecosm,* which is how we crossed paths. I often wondered why he dumped gross national products for gigabytes, until I realized that his new love drove his former.

We sat near the door at a fun restaurant in Palo Alto; knowing George, I had brought along a bottle of 1986 La Mission Haut-Brion to sharpen his mind and loosen his tongue. I was after an economics lesson and a bottle of Bordeaux was cheap compared to what I hoped to extract. Supply and demand, my ass.

"Hey, George, what brings you out this way?" I asked.

"The usual. I've got meetings. Some start-ups, nanotubes, graphics processors, patent analytics . . . you know."

It's always a slow start with George. I lifted the bottle and poured him a small taste. His eyes rolled back slightly as he sipped. I had him.

"You can almost see wealth being created as you drive around here, cathedrals of silicon and towers of bandwidth reaching for the sky." George paused and looked at me. "What's up with you?"

"Economics."

"Drop it."

"I guess it doesn't always make sense."

"Scarcely."

"I just don't get it, George. I've taken macro- and microeconomics. They taught me about supply and demand curves and that where they cross is the right price and that economics is about allocating scarce resources."

"Empty your mind of such nonsense," he replied, taking another sip. "They taught you wrong. Those curves imply a moral and material equivalence between the two curves. It just isn't so. The supply curve is the product of work and creativity exerted over time. The process of creating new supplies creates the initial pattern of demand, which ramifies through the economy. All the market surveys and consumer preferences are phantoms compared to the launching of a new product that surprises people with new capabilities that they couldn't imagine before and spurs them to provide their own work in exchange."

I twiddled my iPhone in my hand, itching to check for new e-mails, until it kicked in what George was talking about. I'd had no idea I wanted an iPhone until I saw an iPhone and worked enough to afford one. Things like iPhones are what make me want to earn enough to afford them.

"The value of money," he went on, "comes not from what people want but from what productive things they do. The demand curve is the reflection of short-term responses that are given meaning only by the demander's previous productive efforts. No way they're equivalent. Supply creates demand—you know that, it's Say's law. It was invented in France in the nineteenth century, like this Haut-Brion."

He took another sip, and I refilled his glass, I know about Say's law. Jean-Baptiste Say (1767–1832), businessman, economist, and pre-Internet futurist perhaps? He coined the word *entrepreneur*, so curse him every time you try to type that on a keyboard. I hate clinging to ideas from dead economists, but Say's law is pretty simple and it holds true: supply constitutes demand. Sometimes it is misstated as "supply creates its own demand"—which is how John Maynard Keynes referred to it—but that's not right. Even George got tripped up. It's more of a "supply represents demand for other stuff." Say said that "a product is no sooner created than it, from that instant, affords a market for other products to the full extent of its own value." And David Ricardo said of Say, "The shoemaker when he exchanges his shoes for bread has an effective demand for bread." Knowing bread exists means the shoemaker busts his hump to make shoes to be able to afford the bread. A little easier grasp than that marginal cost/marginal utility stuff from those dreadfully boring economics lectures.

George must have read my mind. "Forget everything they taught you. It's worthless in the real world. Instead, think of it this way: defining every economic era is a canonical abundance, marked by the plummeting price of a key factor of production. That's the new supply that drives . . ."

"Abundance? Like . . ."

"Wood, coal, oil, silicon, bandwidth, transistors, nanotubes, sunlight, bioinformation, industry standard software, whatever. The abundance or supply changes the economy, and puts both nations and economies through a technological wringer. A new invention radically reduces the price of a key commodity and causes an industrial revolution, in which every competitive business must wring out the residue of the old costs from all its products and practices."

Quite a few folks have been quoting George on abundance and scarcity. *Wired*'s Chris Anderson riffed an entire book about things being Free based on George's ideas. But I was more interested in the changes it brings to wealth creation. "Economies go through a wringer?" I asked.

"Yes." His hands and arms started moving in an up-and-down motion as he spoke; I hoped he wouldn't knock over his wineglass like he did the last time I bought him wine. "Going through the wringer means wasting the cheap resource to exploit the scarce resource."

His glass tips. Uh, oh, there goes the wine.

"You waste wine to get rare vintage ideas." George chuckled.

"Wasting?" I replied, mopping up the spill with my napkin. "That sounds so, uh, wasteful."

"Yes, yes. Waste away what's abundant to make up for what's scarce."

George went on, "Waste is virtuous. From the nucleus of the atom to the sun, energy is infinitely abundant. Except for politics, it would be as dirt cheap as the sand in microchips. Just as we waste energy transforming beach sand into refined silicon ingots and the refined ingots into labyrinthine microchips, we waste energy prodigally when we refine our crude energy into targeted and transformed electricity and information to be delivered to refrigerators, iPods, automobile engines, light bulbs, computer screens, and MRI machines."

I was scrambling to keep up, but my mind kept wandering to all the things we really do waste, from water to oil to electricity, so we can do things that weren't possible before. But if it's abundant, I kept thinking, it must be worthless, right?

"We use most of our energy refining energy and throwing away energy in the form of heat." This snapped me back to attention. He'd obviously thought this through. "The more we wastefully refine energy, the more useful it becomes and the more we use it, and the cheaper the ultimate functionality it delivers. The supply of refined energy creates demand throughout the economy."

"So you're telling me to find what's abundant to make up for what is scarce?" I asked. "That doesn't make sense. I'd always figured that if something is abundant it's by definition cheap and therefore worthless. But you're somehow implying that it has value? If something is scarce, either you find more or it stays scarce. I'm confused again. Damn, seven years of college down the drain?"

"Hey, none of us learned much in college. If the teachers knew much they would be in business. Colleges are increasingly dominated by obscurantist parasites. Engineering and math, though, have utility, and their professors do spend much of their time in business."

I have a brighter opinion of universities, but I've got to keep George on track. "So . . . waste?"

"The more you waste, the better. What's abundant is cheap—the price signal tells you to waste it. What's scarce is expensive. Instead of using economics to allocate what's scarce, just waste something else until what you want is no longer scarce."

"Okay." I nodded and poured a little more wine. I didn't want to "waste" George until I got more out of him.

"Today the cheap resources are bandwidth and computation. The scarce resource is time, which always becomes scarce as other things become abundant, and the human genius that can transcend the scarcity of time."

"Okay, I get that. But when I got to Wall Street, I learned that investors love to buy stock in companies with pricing power, the ones that can raise prices whenever they want to, you know, like utilities and banks and cereal makers. I felt like an idiot for focusing on technology because, in the end, it's just another commodity, right?"

"Everything is eventually a commodity within its own market. That's what markets do. The question is how you define the market. The goal of every business is to raise the volume and predictability of its output to the point that it becomes a commodity. This is achieved not by raising prices but by lowering prices and benefiting from the learning curve efficiencies that result from larger volumes. The largest profits and barriers to entry come when the learning curve is steeper than the curve of declining prices. The issue of intellectual property and its ownership is separate from the issue of commoditization. The most profitable companies launch a large number of learning curves and commodities."

Whoa. There's a lot there to chew on. Profits are best when costs drop faster than prices, as long as prices are dropping. Okay, I get that. Intellectual property—and I guess he means patents and copyrights—can slow how fast prices go down. This can be good for profits but not necessarily good for customers who love falling prices. And yes, the most profitable companies do this again and again.

George is right. I've lived this lowering-costs ideal my whole life. At first without realizing it, I've always been attracted to things that get cheaper over time. Growing up middle class, without access to a lot of things I wanted, it was only natural I'd want them to be cheaper. Did this lead to a more general desire to democratize those things limited to the privileged few? Yeah, maybe.

Of course, there was also the thrill of a challenge. My high school friend Dave Bell and I wanted access to our school's computers so we could play games on them. Denied, we decided to build our own. Yeah, I know, how quaint. We scrapped together a Z-80 microprocessor-based homebrew computer, and even thought of starting a company to sell it. Something about college got in the way, but we each had our own system, wrote programs for it, played games on it, impressed chicks with it. Well, except that last part.

I complained earlier that no one told me what would happen over the years with computers and technology becoming ubiquitous. I had to find out for myself.

I realize now that it was the abundance of transistors, like the ones inside the chips in our homebrew computers, that drove personal computers from one-off hacks like ours (the lights in the house would dim when we reset them, annoying the heck out of my dad, so we had to carefully write code that didn't crash!) to the hundreds of millions that move out the door now, plus all the computing power in cell phones and GPS units and, heck, just about everything else.

According to George, all I really had to do was look for an oncoming abundance and I'd be on the path to success. Turns out I had already found one, but I'd had no clue at the time. Again, just a small whisper in my ear by someone back then would have been quite useful.

As I mentioned earlier, Dave and I worked for AT&T Bell Labs after college, where I was in that group, buried under twenty layers of management, that helped design modems for computer communication. Mostly I wanted one for myself, at home, so I could sleep in and pretend I was at work. The abundance of ever-faster wires and cables and fiber optic links and wireless spectrum now connects all of us. Don't get me wrong, I'm not sitting here trying to impress you that I had some master plan—"oh, just chased era-defining abundance to rid the world of scarcities"—it was just me pursuing my own selfish "I gotta have that" interests. Still, with a little forethought . . .

Same thing for high finance. I worked on Wall Street just as lower trading commissions democratized the bull market beyond banks and pension funds. Fixed 75-cent-per-share commissions began evaporating after Wall Street's Big Bang of 1975, which brought negotiated commissions. Lower inflation kick-started the bull market, but it was individuals paying 25-cent commissions, then 12-cent, then 6-cent commissions on their way to a penny-per-share net that provided the steam to drive it ever higher. TI sold calculators, Intel sold microprocessors, Motorola sold StarTAC cell phones. It was the abundance of those transistors that got things cheap enough to change entire industries, and I found myself smack dab in the middle of it.

Once I started running a hedge fund, I thought about this abundance thing all the time, though we used different terms. My partner and I would wake up every day and ask where bandwidth was getting cheaper, who was making it more abundant, what new products didn't make sense now but would in a few years with greater bandwidth, who is going to get killed? And all before break-fast. With a little forethought, anyone can figure out what will be abundant. Not necessarily zero cost, just headed toward zero over the next few decades.

I suspected George had just revealed to me the key ability of a Free Radical—finding what's abundant. The abundant waster is the one creating wealth.

But wasting what?

Maybe George knows.

"How do you know which ones, which abundant things become important?" I asked.

"The test of abundance is a rapidly declining price, which implies a rising crest of learning. The crucial economic question is whether the learning grows faster than the price, yielding increasing profits, or more slowly, yielding a decline in profits."

Makes sense. Intel processors got cheaper at a faster rate than their prices went down. Apple iPhones are getting better and better while the costs to make them keep dropping faster than prices. When that stops, the game stops and it's time to find another one.

"So I just close my eyes and trust that something that gets cheaper and cheaper increases the value of something else?"

"Yes. But I wouldn't close your eyes. You'll miss the transition from one era to the next. And usually, the winner is the one driving costs down that learning curve. Or working close and leveraging someone else doing it. It doesn't happen on its own. The magic of abundance creates productivity, and wealth comes to those who create it, but it doesn't happen if you sit around and just think something will be more abundant, you often have to make it happen."

Cheap servers and ubiquitous bandwidth made Facebook possible in 2005 versus 1995, but someone had to go out and create it.

"But what about now? In this whole new century thing, we've moved from scarce physical assets to scarce human characteristics, like time and memory and speed of execution and, I don't know—" George was watching people come and go from the restaurant— "maybe attention span?" I quickly poured more wine. My bad. "Are human brain waves abundant or scarce?"

He took a long sip of the Bordeaux. "The chief scarcities are human ingenuity and time. They are what become scarce when everything else becomes abundant. As bandwidth and computation become more abundant, for example, they can compensate for the scarcity of time and some human functions."

I could tell his attention was wandering; it was time to change the subject before I lost him completely.

"So I'm headed back for my college reunion."

"You're wasting your time."

"Why?"

"I have a rule of thumb for reunions."

"What's that?"

"At the fifth college reunion, it's the lawyers who are kings. They're out of law school a few years with jobs at New York law firms. They're driving brand-new foreign cars and wearing custom suits while everyone else is still struggling to figure out what they're going to do."

"Go on."

"At the ten-year, everyone ignores the lawyers; they just look tired and they're usually already divorced. It's the doctors' reunion. They've done their med school and internships and fellowships, maybe even specialized. They have a thriving practice at some prestigious hospital or research center. They tell fascinating stories about saving lives and going to Africa to vaccinate poor children. It's their time to shine."

"Even though they all eventually end up hating it?"

"Yeah, that's at the next few reunions, if they bother coming. They're overworked and their compensation constantly goes down and they're probably taking a few too many self-prescribed medications and—"

"So then who?"

"Well, maybe around the fifteenth it's the financiers, the Wall

Street types. But no one likes them. They call them money changers behind their backs. It's at the twentieth that things get interesting, because then it's the entrepreneurs who shine. Someone who's figured out how to turn dust into gold, created some gotta-have business application or bioengineered some drug or created a business process that transforms retail—"

"And so it's their turn for the spotlight?" I ask.

"You would think. But lots of people who still work for big companies or the government can't get their arms around entrepreneurs. They got rich, too rich, so many people just assume they were lucky or had some monopoly or somehow stole the money from working stiffs who bought their stuff."

"Jealousy?"

"Sure, people are jealous. But they're also programmed to suspect anyone who has done well from taking too big a piece of the pie. Like the pie was taken out of their mouths. They don't realize that these guys made the pie bigger. It's those successful entrepreneurs who created wealth for everyone else in the room. Not the lawyers, not the doctors, not the finance guys, but the creators. Yet they end up getting grief. Go figure."

"Because they're scarce?" I chuckle.

"Very good," George responded. I wasn't sure if he meant my joke or the wine. Didn't matter, though. I'd gotten what I wanted.

A Free Radical finds Gilder's abundance. Every era is defined by something that's abundant. Find it, make sure the invention that you want Scales, and then Waste away.

When in Doubt, Get Horizontal

YOU CAN'T JUST GRAB HOLD OF ANYTHING THAT SCALES and expect to build a business that grows and grows. How you attack a market makes a difference, especially markets filled with entrenched, old-line, milking-it-for-all-it's-worth players who are content to squeeze every last ounce of profits out of a business without growing it or building anything new for their customers. I'm talking about phone companies and broadcasters and hospitals and drug companies and electric utilities and more.

I had an old college roommate named Franz who, after taking business classes, would come back to our house, pound a few beers, and proclaim, "Dude, when in doubt, get horizontal!" Then he'd pass out in front of the TV. Sometimes life lessons come from the strangest places. Franz had revealed the secret of how to really Scale. Getting horizontal is how a Free Radical takes those entrenched, vertically integrated giants out at the knees. Horizontal really means doing something better than anyone else and inserting yourself into a product or process by having someone else do everything else.

SINCE, I DON'T know, Caesar, Alexander, Nebuchadnezzar, we have lived in a world of command and control. Kings, queens, knights, and pawns have given way to presidents, vice presidents, associate vice presidents, assistants to the regional manager, and pawns. Always pawns.

That command-and-control, 120-floors-to-the-executive-suite, vertical corporation is a relic of the Industrial Revolution. Vertical corporations do everything, soup to nuts. Ford had an auto factory, River Rouge, that took iron ore in at one end and spit cars out the other. Why give up profits to your suppliers when you can do everything yourself and capture them all? The do-it-all corporation ruled. But when technology proliferated, that stopped working. Markets scale to enormous proportions. You can't efficiently do everything yourself. Especially when the products became digital bits instead of huge chunks of steel. Scaling to a million customers became a royal pain. Worse, internal politics overvalued each step along the way, as individual section managers would mark up the price on their output so they could collect nice bonuses even though the entire company was going to lose money.

The computer industry used to be a vertical behemoth. Before the PC, IBM did everything from system architecture to software design, manufacturing chips, assembling boards, slapping them in boxes, writing software and applications and packing up the mainframes, and selling them through their very own sales organization—and all the salespeople were expected to service the machines themselves. Soup to nuts or chip to ship—IBM controlled the whole thing. Why not? Why give up profits to someone on the outside when you can capture it for the centrally controlled enterprise?

It was the model of efficiency—five-year plans and all (just like that other model of efficiency in the 1970s, the Soviet Union). Once customers were set up with IBM mainframes, the switching costs were high, so companies would pay whatever IBM asked. Eventually, IBM lost touch entirely with price, overvaluing their mainframes until a huge opening existed for minicomputers, servers, and even personal computers. They unwittingly unleashed the horizontal model that would destroy them, going outside Big Blue for parts for the IBM Personal Computer (a toy that internal projections had selling 250,000 units over five years—oops, it was millions). Intel processors, Microsoft operating system, Western Digital disk controllers.

Same with the old AT&T. They manufactured phones, leased them to customers, ran long distance lines, built switches, and ran wires to homes. Again, soup to nuts; why give up profits to someone else when you can capture it all for yourself? AT&T did IBM one better—they claimed a natural monopoly. After all, what purpose is there in running more than one set of wires to each home? They were regulated by the Federal Communications Commission, which approved rates as a reasonable return on investment, which meant the more they invested, even wasted, the higher their profits. I worked there. I know. AT&T could waste better than anyone.

Inevitably, these vertical monsters failed. IBM and AT&T may have captured the profits from mainframes and telephone calls, but there was a much bigger computer and communications business that they missed. They could have gotten horizontal, given up near-term profits but unleashed a huge growth business. But they didn't. Like railroads forgetting they were in the transportation business instead of the track-laying business, they forgot about price and outsiders took them out at the knees.

Want a more modern example? Look at Sandy Weill's Citigroup. By combining Citibank retail and commercial banking with Travelers insurance and Salomon Brothers brokerage and investment banking, Weill hoped to create a "financial supermarket." In the end, no one really wanted one-stop shopping for financial stuff; you could get the best of whatever you wanted from horizontal competitors or even on the Internet, your own personal, virtual supermarket. When profits proved elusive, Citigroup speculated in real estate loans to make money. How dumb was that? The stock dropped from $50 to $3.

The digital world is made up of discrete layers of highly valued scalable intellectual property, not the complete finished product that generates returns on capital for a vertically integrated organization. It makes a big difference.

Intel makes the processors (wasting transistors), Microsoft writes the operating system (wasting bits), Hewlett-Packard puts together a motherboard and puts plastic around it and sells it at Best Buy. And there are probably two or three dozen other interesting slivers of intellectual property in there as well, in the disk drive, the graphics, even the power supply.

Same with cell phones: Qualcomm and others design the chips, which are manufactured in Taiwan. Nokia and Motorola sell the phones, while Verizon and AT&T run the service. Apple's iPhone design is assembled by Inventec and other companies in China. HTC makes phones that run Google's Android operating system.

A natural food chain comprising horizontal layers of intellectual property is the new modern structure replacing the vertical corporation. Horizontal is both efficient and the best structure to generate profits. Wall Street, by feeding those that it believes can generate returns, and starving those that can't, is the ultimate arbiter of this sweeping change.

Horizontal is better than vertical because it harnesses separate layers of innovation, something the vertical model makes almost impossible. It sounds odd, but a partnership between two profit-driven enterprises is usually more manageable and productive than the relationship between two divisions of a large company, each of whose VP wants to be CEO someday. Vertical phone company giants like AT&T saw their growth taken away by horizontals like Level 3 and Skype; the PC business all over again.

ON THE SURFACE, a horizontal structure is counterintuitive. For instance, one good reason to integrate vertically is supply. When there are long, slow supply lines, or unsure supplies of key inputs, it makes sense to integrate vertically to make up for the lack of certainty. Put it all under your control to guarantee supplies, as Ford did with the River Rouge plant. The British Empire colonized much of the world to lock up the supply of raw materials (to feed their factories, and keep them out of French and German hands).

But the reason a horizontal structure is the most efficient is twofold: price and pace.

Prices are set by the marketplace. IBM was segmented in divisions that were supposedly independent, but one group would "sell" their output to the next at some phony transfer price, showing a "profit." Every division might show a profit, but the company itself would still lose money because, in the real world, someone else sold the product more cheaply, which meant that competitors could get the same thing done for a lot less (and pass the savings along in the form of lower prices). I saw this when I worked at AT&T. We used to design and sell modem chips to Western Electric for $30, about three times what it cost us to make—a tidy "profit." They would put it on a board and manufacture modems and sell them to the sales division for $100, another nice markup, showing a "profit" in doing so. The sales division would mark it up to $200 and try to sell it in the marketplace—and fall on its face, because Hayes and USRobotics and others were selling the same modems for $79. My boss got a bonus for the success of our division, but the company lost a fortune. Duh.

Meanwhile, in a horizontal ecosystem, innovation in one layer can accelerate at its own pace without holding back the others. For instance, chip design today moves faster than operating system design. Intel turns out new processors every two to three years, while Microsoft releases new versions of Windows closer to every five to seven years. In a vertical company, the processor guys have to wait around for the software guys while their competitors continue improving steadily.

When you get horizontal, you can come up with the greatest innovation in your layer and slip it into the market, letting the other layers adapt to you, rather than letting them slow down the whole system. Other layers of the stack can Scale, even if yours doesn't. Sometimes that's not a bad strategy, glomming onto and riding someone else's Scale and Waste. Microsoft kept raising prices for Windows while Intel constantly increased the performance and lowered the price of their processors in PCs.

■   ■   ■

THE OTHER REASON to go horizontal, to own some sliver of intellectual property in a layer of a horizontal stack, is that it's the easiest way to enter a market. Rather than building factories or hiring a huge sales force, you just license your crucial piece of intellectual property to others. They drop it into the stack and go on their way. It might be a piece of code, a chip, a design process, or a key piece of biopharma, whatever. Create it, protect it, and then turn it sideways and fit it into the industry's horizontal stack. Or into someone's existing vertical business—just find the gap where your stuff fits in. Let another company, or many other companies, do all the hard work of making it, selling it, servicing it, and so on. Owning a sliver is the way to insinuate yourself into the next big thing without having to build a giant vertical behemoth.

Whenever I look at companies, I try to figure out how horizontal they are. Some signs that companies are leaning vertical:

1. They insist on designing everything themselves

2. They build a huge sales force

3. They compete with everyone in the industry, rather than partner

4. They build their own stores (like Apple)

5. They piss and moan when you accuse them of being vertical

HEY, WAIT A second, you're thinking. Apple is a huge success with their iPhone and iPad and they're vertically integrated: they have their own stores, their own operating system, and a closed-system architecture to capture more of their own profits.

Not so fast. Apple doesn't manufacture anymore. Their devices are assembled by other companies in Taiwan and China; they've eliminated that layer. For the most part, they don't make their own chips. They do design a few of them, but not all of them, and others manufacture the chips. Yes, Apple is maniacal about their operating system, keeping it closed, but they do allow others to write applications. Today, the number of third-party mobile apps in their online store is a huge differentiator, with billions of downloads in 2010. Early reviews of a wannabe competitor, the Palm Pre, pointed to the lack of apps for the device. Outside manufacturers like Belkin offer all sorts of Apple accessories, from laptop stands to iPhone cases. And the Apple Stores are as much a marketing campaign to make you feel good about buying (and overpaying for) Apple products as a drive for verticality. So yes, Apple is more vertical than the Windows/Intel world, but mainly in areas of controlling the experience rather than capturing profits. Still, if I were them, I'd be just a little bit nervous about a true horizontal competitor, such as Google, outrunning them.

Vertical is an end-of-life-cycle business structure, not appropriate at all for Free Radicals looking to create massive growth. Of course, that doesn't mean you can't make a lot of money going vertical, for yourself anyway. I was at a dinner in Chicago for a consumer software company providing medical information on CDs. This was just as the Internet came along and the info became available for free on the Web. I forget the company; they were boring and dull and ultimately failed. But I remember that a bunch of investors in the company were at my table, many of whom had the same last name: Pritzker, as in the wealthy Chicago hotel and industrial company Pritzker. Nice folks.

One of them was talking about mining, so I started paying attention because the medical company was so awfully dull. The family either owned mines or operated mines or owned mining equipment. Hey, they knew a lot about mines. One of the uncles had been working the mining business for a bunch of years when he realized that if the family owned both the company that drilled the stuff out of the mines as well as the company that transported the coal or ore or whatever out of the mines, then maybe they could make more money. One of the young Pritzkers put it quite simply: they made a fortune.

All I could think about for the next few weeks was how could I find things to vertically integrate, because, heck, if the Pritzkers could make a fortune, or yet another fortune, maybe I had a shot at it. It took another few weeks to realize that the only reason their vertical integration deal worked is that mining is a no-innovation, no-excitement, no-Scale, not-much-growth kind of business. No one is writing code to improve mining. There is nothing to scale by a factor of ten, let alone thousands. You couldn't get the engines to rev faster or lower the costs by half every few years. It's a dead business, innovation-wise, and therefore not spitting out any more increases in living standards for society. So you almost have to vertically integrate it to squeeze out more profits. And the Pritzkers did. But then again, they're not Free Radicals.

THINKING VERTICAL VERSUS horizontal is always on my mind.

"HEADED HOME?"

"Yup." I'm on a plane. I've just spent thirty-six hours in New York, a quick tactical strike with a dozen meetings and a way too late dinner and wine and cask-strength Laphroaig and all I want to do is pass out and wake up somewhere over Nebraska, read the paper, listen to some tunes, and get home so I can go back to sleep.

"I love San Francisco . . ."

"Uh-huh." Pause. Oh crap, he wants more. "You headed home as well?" I reluctantly ask.

"Oh no, just making my way back. I'm down in LA. Ventura, actually. My wife is meeting me up in San Fran for a few nights. Our kids are off to school, so she tries to meet me when she can."

"That's nice." Pleasant fellow, I decide. Looks pretty young to have kids in college. His face is slightly tanned, but there's not a hint of lines or wrinkles or aging.

"You in Pacific Heights?" he asks.

"Oh, no, I live down in the Peninsula, near Palo Alto."

"Been there tons. Epicenter of Silicon Valley. You in the tech business?"

"Sort of. More of a writer now."

"Now?"

"I do some investing, but now mostly write stuff."

"Oh, like what?" Jeez. The Laphroaig isn't making me any friendlier.

"I wrote a book on medicine . . ."

"Oh."

Pause.

So I continue. "Silicon Valley and chips for early detection of cancer or heart disease that will destroy doctors. That's the Cliffs-Notes version anyway."

"Oh, how neat. I'm sort of in the medical business myself. My company anyway. Prevention."

"Uh-huh."

"Yeah, it's the strangest thing. We just won innovation of the year at a medical conference and we don't sell drugs or devices or anything like that. You use suntan lotion?"

"Sure."

"Every day?"

"No."

"But you should, right? Skin cancer is a big problem, especially out in California. But you don't. No one does."

"That's true."

"Too greasy, right?"

"Yeah, too greasy and too messy to apply."

"We've got this guy who figured out how to attach a tiny electrical charge to things, just enough to get it to attract and attach to other things, like your skin."

"Like rubbing a balloon on your shirt and sticking it to your head?"

"Exactly. So we took his process and applied it to sunblock. Instead of slathering the SPF compounds in grease to get it to stick to your skin, we just charge it with our process and then embed it in soaps and shampoos and lotions."

I sit up in my seat. This is the coolest thing (without a chip in it) I've heard about in a while.

"And it works?"

"Oh, sure. It lasts about a day, which is longer than regular sunblock, and it doesn't come off when you swim. And it's not greasy. You don't even know you have it on. Just take a shower and you're covered. We have a factory that turns out the charged compound; it's pretty cheap to make."

"So you're going to license it, right?" Own the horizontal. Who wouldn't buy Dove soap with SPF 50 built in?

"We're talking to everyone, but we've decided to make our own branded soap."

"Oh." Pause. "Don't you want to brand it, sell it to all takers?"

"Probably not."

"So you're going to build your own sales force to sell this."

"We're raising money right now to do that."

"Well, that's exciting. Quite a challenge . . ."

I don't know this guy well enough to tell him he needs to get horizontal. But let's face it, he does. First of all, manufacturing anything that touches your body has to go through all sorts of inspections and testing and regulations and, not knowing much about soap sales, I'm pretty sure there are only a handful of companies that just make up names to sell the same product with different shapes and scents. Dove, Dial, Irish Spring, Ivory.

Procter & Gamble and Colgate-Palmolive have entire office parks stocked with marketers dreaming up new ways to convince us to buy more of the same soap. Teeming hordes of salespeople descend on Walmarts and supermarkets and drugstores, combing the aisles to make sure their brand has the best placement. Alarms would go off in headquarters if anyone even tried to encroach on their hard-won shelf space. Yikes. I get lightheaded even thinking about it. Maybe it's the altitude. Or the Laphroaig.

"Our investors think we should go for it," he continues. "Build a big business that we can expand to other markets. We didn't want to just create a company that collects royalty checks every month. It's too easy to get cut off."

"Can't you sell the secret SPF juice to other companies?"

"Sure, we can do anything. But for now, we're trying to maximize revenue."

Drinks come by and we chitchat about California and families and schools until I look so tired he backs off and lets me sleep.

But I can't get out of my head that here's an entrepreneur with a hot, hot, hot idea headed up the vertical climb and building out a giant company just so he can sell soap rather than lie down on his side and get horizontal. What a shame. He could have been a contender.

WHEN IN DOUBT, a Free Radical gets horizontal!

Intelligence Moves Out to the Edge of the Network

IT'S NOT JUST THAT COMPUTERS GET CHEAPER EVERY YEAR or that communication gets cheaper every year—it's also a proliferation thing. These tiny little chips show up all over the place, helping you and me make calls, listen to music, take photos, navigate in our cars, figure out if a cornfield needs to be irrigated—even set the spark timing in our Hemi engines. Scale is just the first-order effect. What happens when these little programmable things are everywhere? Can a Free Radical take advantage of this proliferation of devices and code?

Command-and-control organizations are a dying breed, but what will replace them? Chaos? Hardly. The next stage has become a mantra in Silicon Valley: Intelligence moves out to the edge of the network.

Burn it into your brain. It's the architecture for Free Radicals.

When you put all these smart devices out there, magical things happen. Until now, networks have been things like phone networks, lots of smarts in switches inside the phone companies and a dumb phone with twelve gray buttons on your desk. To do call forwarding took several years of reengineering and reprogramming those switches to get them to talk to each other. Voice mail? Forget it, a nightmare. Or let's look at the TV networks. A giant transmitter on top of the Empire State Building or a cable operator blasts shows indiscriminately to dumb TVs equipped with a channel selector. You can say the same thing about credit card processing. Or health care. Or government.

But now, with ever-cheaper communications, Internet packets pass through routers from Cisco and move all the information we would ever want to wherever we want. These routers are complicated pieces of equipment that, in a sense, created a really dumb network. We don't expect these routers to think, just to get what we want from one side of the network to the other. E-mail, Web pages, phone calls, video, Twitter tweets, whatever. The beauty of a dumb network is that the intelligence on the edge can invent new stuff, like new applications, any time it wants.

The edge of the network is your computer or phone or even servers sitting in a data center. That's where the intelligence exists, not in the system that moves things around. Transport of information (in the form of packets) stays dumb so that the devices on the edge of the network can get smarter and smarter and take that information and do new and exciting things not yet imagined. This trend of intelligence at the edge is unstoppable.

Voice mail, for instance. Just record voice to a disk drive and play it back off a Web page. Better yet, transcribe it and send me an e-mail. I can't live without this, since I never have to talk to anyone on the phone. I now just reply to an e-mail of their voice! Or getting my desk phone and my cell phone to ring at the same time and the call ending up on the phone I pick up, which Google Voice implements at the edge. Need something like TiVo? Record video to a hard drive. Or stream it like Hulu and Netflix. And I'll program it, not Jeff Zucker at NBC. Three-way calling? Just send my packets to a few places instead of one. Nine-way calling? Simple.

There is no voice anymore. Or music. Or TV shows or magazines or movies; there is just data. As soon as Free Radicals reconfigure their brains around data instead of the shape data takes (or used to take), you can begin to figure out what's happening at the edge.

Think about Google. For all the talk of giant data centers with zillions of servers, which sure as heck sounds like the center of the network, Google is the number one beneficiary of intelligence at the edge of the network. It's the transport of data to and from those data centers that stays dumb. Our desktop computers and laptops and smartphones on the edge aren't going away, but as bandwidth speeds increase, more and more computing can be done on the network of computers sitting in data centers—also known as the "cloud." Cloud computing provides search results, processes company payrolls, coordinates video games played by thousands of people simultaneously; even the complex graphics for those games are starting to be drawn in the cloud. Anyone can do it, but it's not cheap. These clouds are multibillion-dollar investments in data centers and fiber optics. The Internet is far from mature, and its growth is an ever more high-stakes game.

Once you build the cloud, it's all about network operations. Whoever can deliver search results faster wins. Users usually only realize this subconsciously, but it's true: Google's dominant share is as much about speed as it is about relevant results. Compare it with

Microsoft or Yahoo! search and you'll see. Google often builds its data centers next to waterfalls so electricity can be cheap enough to help it win the speed war.

New cloud computing applications appear every day—backing up files, managing your money, editing photos, running the back end of multiplayer games like World of Warcraft. Now corporate America is moving its accounting, scheduling, order management, and the like into the cloud, and speed is a top priority.

Now wait one second. I invoke the IGA (the Inevitable Google Analogy—all you have to do is show that Google does something to prove it's the greatest strategy ever!) to prove intelligence is at the edge? Isn't that the exception to the rule, since Google servers are in this so-called cloud?

Nope. I don't want to get too geeky here, but notice I said computing can be done *on* their network of computers, not *in* the network. Google's servers in their data centers are also on the edge of the network, not inside the network. It may sound like semantics, but it makes a difference. Google couldn't care less how their packets get to you (beyond the politics of telcos and cable companies slowing down their packets). Cellular networks to your phone, cable modem to your home PC, fiber to your work laptop, municipal Wi-Fi to your Xbox video games, it doesn't matter.

Think of it this way. Google doesn't create information, they create a sandbox for you and me and everyone else to store and manipulate our information (and watch out for cats who think the sandbox is filled with kitty litter). Or think of them as Tom Sawyer, putting up a picket fence and handing each of us brushes and paint. We do all the work of putting up pages and linking to others. We all are on the edge of the network, but Google was nice enough to put up really fast servers optimized to search and find things.

Google didn't have to enter all the information about what the weather is in Toledo, or the address of Taillevent in Paris, or how to do least mean square calculations. We put that up on our Web sites, and Google helps organize that intelligence at the edge. We did all the work and they get big fat margins selling ads on it.

Google doesn't have to create anything themselves. There is no centralized control. They don't pay Katie Couric to read the news. There are no legions of overcaffeinated, pajama-clad bloggers tickling keyboards on Google's payroll. Another great example of Say's law—supply constitutes demand. We didn't even know we needed search engines and blogs and social networks until someone set them up, and now demand is through the roof.

But remember, Google is nothing without the rest of us. They connect their edge to our edge through the network—but you better believe they are just as much on the edge as their users. That's why it works.

The cloud is nothing without devices, browsers, and stuff to be read or watched or commented on to feed it.

So it's not just about faster processors sitting in phones and TVs and cameras and sneakers; intelligence is just as much about the people attached to those faster processors, where they are, what they are doing, their mood, their interests. The processors are just good at capturing all that cheaply.

Even boring old analog businesses like electric utilities are jumping into intelligence at the edge. Smart thermostats and smart electric meters and programmable charging times for electric vehicles are classic examples of the edge interfacing with people, who save money on their electric bills by letting machines juggle their electricity use. For instance, you might decide to run your dryer at night when the grid is underutilized and rates are lower. I don't want to set the alarm for 2 a.m. to turn the stupid dryer on, but a little intelligent device can do it for me. The more intelligence in all of our devices, the better. By shifting more demand overnight, we can build fewer new power plants to handle peak demand during the day.

Plus, the more sensing of voice and faces and motion and gestures and comfortable temperatures that can be done by all this intelligence at the edge of the network, the better the overall system will perform. So simple: if no one is in the room, turn off the heat.

THERE ARE REAL human beings at the edge. Let them do a lot of the work for you.

Having a fast cloud is useless if you keep it closed. The trick is to open it up as a platform for every new business idea to run on, charging appropriate fees as necessary. I sat through a keynote speech by Bill Gates maybe fifteen years ago. Asked why Microsoft makes all the money in the software business, he snapped: *We don't make all the money. We only make money because we are a platform for others to use our software to make money themselves.*

Only by opening up the system to thousands of hungry developers and users can anyone truly create an operating system in the cloud. Make it Tom Sawyer–like.

Like open-source software, which according to the Open Source Initiative is "a development method for software that harnesses the power of distributed peer review and transparency of process. The promise of open source is better quality, higher reliability, more flexibility, lower cost, and an end to predatory vendor lock-in."

In other words, there are a bunch of folks around the world who write and revise code, for free, for a software project that is open to contributions from anyone. Linux is an open-source operating system. Apache is open-source server software that spits out most Web pages. Firefox is an open-source browser. Successful open-source projects capture value from the project. The Mozilla Foundation cut a deal with Google to include a search toolbar and collects tens of millions in referral fees.

In Sweden, Mårten Mickos tapped programmers around the globe to contribute code and help fix bugs in his MySQL open-source database application. Tom Sawyer again. Let others paint the picket fence. But he also ended up with four hundred employees of his own, many writing proprietary code. He told me once that he had the best of both worlds—a loyal following of coders to enhance his software, but his own protected layers (in effect, horizontal slivers) of code so no one could just copy all of his software and give it away for nothing. The main database might be free, but some of the other tools you need to use it cost money. Pretty smart. He never did put database giant Oracle out of business, but he undercut their prices and opened up a new segment of database users. In early 2008, Mickos ended up selling MySQL to Sun Microsystems for $1 billion. In spring 2009, Sun was sold to Oracle for around $7 billion. This Tom Sawyer thing can be quite valuable!

There have been many attempts to harness the edge in health care too. Privacy is obviously an issue, but the ability to create databases of symptoms and diseases and drugs and side effects can be enormously valuable, with so much of the Intelligence at the Edge, with doctors and especially with patients. The biggest near-term gain will probably be seen by networking researchers. Sage Bionetworks allows researchers around the world to contribute to and draw from an open database of clinical and molecular data so they can "build innovative new dynamic disease models." But it's not just for scientists; 23andMe analyzes your DNA and then compares it with others' to identify your potential predisposition to various diseases. Lots of issues need to be worked out, not the least of which is, what does "your DNA suggests a 27 percent probability of contracting liver cancer" even mean? The Personal Genome Project, meanwhile, lets individuals upload their DNA sequencing for researchers to probe, privacy be damned.

To succeed, you have to live out on the edge, where the intelligence resides. The center is increasingly dumb, out of touch, always trying to catch up to all the great things that are going on at the edge of networks, whether that's electronic networks or plain old people networks. People networks have always been informal. "Hey, what's up? How you doin'? What's happenin'?" Passing by someone's office, passing notes in history class, making phone calls, sending text messages—people have a huge desire to know what other people are doing.

When electronic and people networks overlap, you have social networks. And then things get really interesting.

Social networking is a powerful tool, especially for getting someone else to do work for you. Interviewing Facebook founder Mark Zuckerberg helped me finally make sense of the phenomenon.

"What did you see that got this thing off the ground?" I asked.

"There's this weird effect," he explained. "If you have a lot of people contributing information, a lot of times you can build a source or a set of information that's just better than any individual can do."

I have T-shirts older than Mark Zuckerberg. At the time I met him Facebook probably had a mere 100 million users. He was twenty-two, confident but somewhat soft-spoken. Not one for shouting from the mountaintop.

"I have a funny story that kind of illustrates this," he continued. "I was building Facebook at Harvard during finals period of fall term." Mark shifted in his seat a little bit. I'm sure he was nervous,

but my nerves were jangled, too: I was pretending to be a journalist, interviewing him for an op-ed in the Saturday *Wall Street
Journal*. "There was this class that I just hadn't been to in a while,
it was called 'Rome of Augustus.'" Mark chuckled, perhaps at the
absurdity that he actually took a course about Rome in the time of
Augustus.

"It was basically history, but also an art course. And for the
final exam, one of the things we had to do was learn the historical significance of something like five hundred pieces of art from
that period. And, having not really read that stuff, I was in a lot of
trouble, and I spent my time building Facebook instead of study-
ing that. So what I ended up doing right before the final, I guess
a few days before, I went to the course Web site, downloaded all
the images, made a new Web site, where there was a page for each
image, right, where the image was there and there was a box to add
comments, and then I sent out a link to this site to the class list,
and said, 'Hey, guys, I built a study tool. Everyone just can go use
this to go comment and see what everyone else was commenting
on these photos.'"

Cheating in the computer age. Or was it?

"So within an hour or two, a bunch of people in the class went
and filled out all the information about the photos. I just went back
and kind of absorbed it all. I got an A in the class. I think generally,
I heard something afterwards, that the grades in that class on the
final were way higher than they have ever been."

I started wondering why this wasn't the way most college
courses are taught, instead of trudging through foul weather and
crowding into a lecture hall to listen to an even fouler professor
blast through material so he can go back to his research. I suppose Mark had similar thoughts, since he deferred his studies and
emigrated to Palo Alto—where he had heard technology compa-

nies are often successful—and attracted enough venture capital to launch what quickly became a rocket ship with no bounds.

It's telling that Mark basically improved the productivity of college learning, for "Rome of Augustus" anyway, and then dropped the idea to improve the productivity of relationships. Perhaps he realized that increasing the productivity of learning has no economic value—there is no academic constituency genuinely interested in making it better. The idea of college in three years is blasphemy to a university president.

"So, I mean, I feel like that story," Mark continued, "while it's also funny, also illustrates the power of this stuff. Before, each individual had to go to the textbook to learn all this stuff, but now there is a more efficient and sort of revolutionary way, by taking the understanding that all the individuals have and pooling that knowledge together, you get a better set of knowledge and just a better solution to the problem. I kind of feel that that's what we are doing here, but instead of being 'what is the historical significance of a small set of images' it's 'What's going on in the world with these people that I care about?'

"'And instead of trying somehow to figure out what's going on with them, you just create a set of tools that allows them to share whatever information they want and then the solution just becomes apparent, because everyone shared what's going on with them and now I can just go to the site easily and just absorb what's going on with all these people and . . . that's cool."

"And you think this will continue to scale?" I ask.

"What we are doing is lowering the cost of communications between people. Not by lowering the cost of a phone call or anything, but by changing the interface, making it easier for people to stay up to date, keep in touch, without the time-consuming problem of actually talking."

That's his abundance, I realized. Wasting storage and band-width and using data to lower the cost of communications, in ways never before possible. That's the economic case for Facebook. You won't find it in Econ 101, but it's there. Productivity. Time saved communicating and finding information. There is some value to that: $20 per hour? Who knows? Facebook isn't going to charge that. But that's their economic value. Instead, they are selling ads, much like Google. But anytime you lower costs, good things happen.

Facebook is at the edge, but it's also a good model of waste and scale and probably more. No wonder it's become ubiquitous. Sell-ing advertising may not be the ultimate business for Facebook; only time will tell. But Zuckerberg is a classic Free Radical, creating a structure for wealth not only for himself but also for society, by lowering the cost of communications, or at least some new form of communications. He has used all of the Rules I've laid out so far and I'd bet dollars to donuts he uses or will use the rest of the Rules too. Later in life, he'll probably be judged by what diseases he tries to eradicate or how much he donates to Africa. But forget it—he's already done his share.

NURTURE THE EDGE. If you don't want to think about it as Tom Sawyer getting his fence painted by providing paint and brushes to his friends, think about it as a sandbox. Free Radicals create a sandbox for others to play in. Sit back. Add more sand when necessary.

Once everyone is playing in the sandbox, then it's time to har-vest what they do.

Wealth Comes from Productivity; Everything Else Is Gravy

IN THE FIRST PART OF 2010, IN AN OP-ED FOR *THE WALL STREET Journal,* I wrote, "It's been ten long years since the economy has created real wealth, as opposed to easy-credit-induced real estate or paper wealth." I got tons of responses, but one e-mail stuck out, from a guy named James:

> Do you have any suggestions on reading or other background on the concept of what "real wealth" is? I'm not sure Adam Smith addressed it, and I don't think my business school (Chicago) did either.

Now James may have been pulling my chain, subtly telling me I had no idea what I was talking about and that Adam Smith and the Chicago Booth School are the sources of all things economic. Or maybe he was pushing me to explain. So here it goes:

Saul Alinsky had his Rules for gaining power. And with power come wealth, or at least the power to redistribute wealth. But what is real wealth in the first place? How do you create it? The simple answer is productivity. But just because it's simple doesn't mean it's easy or obvious.

We humans have needs: water, food, shelter, clothing, and ESPN in HD. It's all basic survival.

If it were just you, living by a lake and pulling out a couple of fish a day, things probably wouldn't be so hard. You fend for yourself the best you can. But as soon as some folks move into the neighborhood, you run into problems. Now you might actually have to do some work. Maybe you're not so good at building huts or killing bears for stylish winter coats. You offer to fish for the new folk if they agree to do all that other stuff for you. Voilà, specialization is born.

A little bit later, you decide you want a larger hut, with a big bearskin rug. How are you going to pay your fellow villagers for all that work on a couple of fish a day? Hmm. You notice some sinewy tree branches, weave them into a net (man, aren't you a genius), and now you're pulling in two dozen fish a day out of the lake. Woohoo. You become the world's first Maker. Your output per day or per hour just went up big-time. That's productivity.

People from all over want to trade you things for all those delicious fish. Eventually, you stop fishing altogether, spending your time weaving fish nets. People from all over flock to your lakeshore palace to buy these newfangled devices. You charge them a third of their yearly "fish catch equivalent." If only someone would invent money so these Neanderthals would quit dumping dead fish in your house!

You get rich, meaning your standard of living goes up. No more cold winter nights for you with your bearskin rugs and big stone fireplace. But everyone who buys your nets also gets rich at their own lakes. Even the people who ultimately trade for actual fish see an increase in their living standards because they don't have to sit around all day fishing; they can spend more time designing bear traps or other newfangled innovations.

All productivity, all the time.

I don't want to do a whole economics lesson of the butcher and baker and candlestick maker and the lovely benefits of free trade. Go read Adam Smith or something. I just want to remind you (and myself) that it's all about productivity.

According to the Economic Policy Institute, "Labor productivity is a measure of the amount of goods and services that the average worker produces in an hour of work. The level of productivity is the single most important determinant of a country's standard of living, with faster productivity growth leading to an increasingly better standard of living."

Increased productivity = better living. Bingo.

Sometimes businesses talk about Economic Value Added—I even catch myself using the expression every once in a while. But EVA is really about profits. Be careful, though: profits can, but don't always, represent productivity.

So we work harder and harder each generation, even though our standard of living has already increased above and beyond the wildest imaginations of previous generations.

According to one MIT study, a modern worker needs to work just eleven hours today to produce as much as a worker putting in a forty-hour workweek in 1950. So we've seen an almost fourfold increase in wealth in sixty years. We could work something like a half hour per week less per year to keep the same standard of living we had in 1950. That's amazing. In other words, tell those who talk about the "good old days" to shut the hell up—our parents worked their butts off for a quarter of what we have today.

But we don't work less. Because who wants last year's or the year before's standard of living? Not me. No cars, no jets, no antibiotics, no heart stents, no laparoscopic surgery, no color TV, no living to eighty-five, no Adult Swim late at night on the Cartoon Network. That's not an interesting world for me. We didn't stop innovating with six-horse wagons or a 1-megahertz PC. We work harder because we actually enjoy our increase in wealth. We work hard selfishly, of course, but all of this new wealth doesn't just end up in the hands of a few fat cats living high on the hog. It's for all of society. A chicken in every pot, two cars in every garage, and ESPN, ESPN2, and ESPN News on every plasma.

Oh, and by the way, lots of people look at wealth and standards of living in different ways. It's easy to get fooled. It is too easy for people to get caught up in the touchy-feely stuff. Let's face it—we don't, except for a few of my neighbors, live in the Caveman Era anymore. So there are plenty of other "needs"—especially in California. In 1943, psychologist Abraham Maslow defined a hierarchy of needs, in ascending order: (1) physiological/biological needs, (2) safety needs, (3) love, affection, and belongingness/social needs, (4) esteem, and (5) self-actualization.

Let others fall into this Maslowian/Feed Your Head trap. Productivity drives living standards and wealth, not actualization—self or otherwise. Don't get caught saying "I need a little me time." While others are scrambling to overcome their shortcomings in affection, a Free Radical finds the next wave of productivity, and all the touchy-feely people will end up working for you. And eventually hold you in high esteem. You win!

■   ■   ■

WHAT ABOUT MACHINES? And capital? What about the money to pay for all these cool new things? Well, it's all intimately related to productivity. Money is not just about keeping score.

A Free Radical has to understand how money works and how productivity is the only way to increase wealth, as opposed to increasing money.

Let's go back to fundamentals for a second. Money is just a placeholder of value—the price of a cold Heineken or the value of work already done, a hole dug, a fish net woven, a piece of software written, whatever. When things work right, prices seek their correct level, and we get a match between that cold beer and the sweat from working for it with money facilitating the swap.

Money supply is how much money is floating around the economy to handle all the transactions. No one quite knows how much money is needed. The classic formula states that the output of the economy equals the amount of money (that the government creates in the form of currency and that banks create via loans) times the velocity of money, or how many times the same dollar is spent during the year. You buy the beer, the bartender stocks up on beer nuts, the nut farmer buys a pickup truck, and the auto worker buys a cell phone, for which you just finished writing the location-based app. You're celebrating by buying a beer. And on and on. Of course, no one really knows what the velocity of money is. If times are tough, you may hold off buying that Heineken for a few months, and when times are good you might party every night.

I like to think of the economy as a bucket filled with money (money supply) sloshing around (velocity). Hopefully, the bucket is filled just to the rim. In normal times, the economy grows as the population increases; the bucket has to get bigger to handle the transactions of more people. So more money needs to be created to fill the bucket.

That's pretty straightforward.

But now the hard part. People are out there inventing useful things, refrigeration, steamships, ATMs—things that increase the output per worker hour. Productivity increases the size and wealth of the economy above and beyond population growth. By how much? Who knows? Economists are notoriously awful at dealing with real numbers. Still, more money needs to be created to fill the bigger bucket. But since no one knows what the velocity of money is, no one knows how much money is needed to keep the economy working just right. So it's virtually impossible to fill the bucket just up to the rim. The Federal Reserve, the U.S. central bank that creates our fiat currency by allowing fractional reserve banks to operate, just guesses and creates what they think is the right amount of money.

As we all know, too much money chasing too few goods creates inflation, a situation where prices go up above and beyond what they normally would if the supply of money and the actual wealth in society were perfectly matched. Too much money means a rising price level. That sucks because you get less stuff for the same unit of work. On the flip side, too little money chasing too many goods and you get deflation, where the price level goes down below what it normally would. Hey, you actually get more for your dollar. Woohoo! Except eventually someone is either going to cut your salary or you'll lose your job because the price level is dropping and the economy is smaller. That sucks too.

Okay, there are many more moving parts than just a simple bucket, including the size of government, its regulations, and not least, the taxing of its citizens/serfs. And I don't just mean income tax, state tax, sales tax, gas tax, property tax . . . one of the easiest ways to "tax" is to debase the currency; just print more and more of it and spend it on chariots and crowns and castles and the Department of Labor. This is why for many, many moons, gold and silver were the money supply. It's the only thing people would trust. The great thing about gold and silver is that they are rare, which means there is only so much of them. New discoveries increase the amount of gold by about 1 percent every year. Hence, you have a stable money supply: with a gold standard, the money supply would grow 1 percent, too, which most economists figured was just right.

But there are a couple of problems with that whole 1 percent thing. The new wealth from more gold goes to the miner who found it, and then it starts circulating in the economy so others can use it. Doesn't seem quite fair. Plus, the 1 percent increase in gold and therefore money supply basically covers population growth, and completely ignores productivity and innovation, which get stifled because there's not enough money to increase output, even with these new tools and inventions. So a gold standard implies a static world. No thanks.

Even without more gold, goldsmiths and money changers learned long ago to hold gold for their clients, maybe even paying them a small interest rate for the privilege of holding their gold, and then to turn around and lend out money (often creating their own bills of currency) backed by that gold. And not one dollar for each one dollar in gold held. No, no, no. They might as well lend out ten times as much money as the gold held, figuring not all "depositors" would want their gold back at the same time. Money from nothing (and your checks for free). Sort of, anyway. This sleight of hand is called fractional reserve banking, and was an easy (if not a little sleazy, no?)

way to increase money supply to, again, make room for productivity and wealth creation. But how much money? No one knows, which is why there were occasionally bank runs and panics and depressions that followed easy credit, one of the hazards of this flimsy system. Sixteen panics since 1812—it's as American as apple pie!

But banking did increase money supply beyond just how much gold could be extracted. In fact, since Adam and Eve, 160,000 tons of gold have been panned and mined from Mother Earth, enough to fill two Olympic-sized swimming pools. At $35 per ounce under the old gold standard, that comes to $180 billion in value, not nearly enough to support all the value created by entrepreneurs. Heck, Google is worth almost that much!

In the long run, the economy grew faster than population, ushering in railroads and interstate highways and even Carrot Top performing at the Luxor in Las Vegas. Now that's wealth. So something eventually went right. One was the Federal Reserve, created in 1913 to control how much money is in circulation. They would create a monetary base, originally backed by the gold in Fort Knox, that private banks would then lend against. Until the United States and others went off gold and declared the value of the dollar by fiat. That is, the dollar is worth a dollar because we say it is. Actually, that's okay, as long as they created just enough of it to match real wealth based on both population growth and productivity.

One of the roles of the Federal Reserve is the lender of last resort, which they unfortunately learned after the stock market crash of 1929 and the bank runs that followed. Ten thousand banks failed, roughly 40 percent, and $2 billion in deposits were wiped out—30 percent of the money supply disappeared. So did a similar percentage of GDP, and unemployment hit 25 percent. You can see that lost money supply is not a good thing.

So the other big change happened twenty years later, in 1933.

The Federal Deposit Insurance Corporation (FDIC) was set up to insure depositors' money, negating the desire for people to line up to get their money out at the first sign of a bank's weakness. No more bank runs. Not many, anyway. (We can argue about whether the FDIC is really an insurance policy, as they undercharge banks for the privilege of insuring against bank runs, and you and I, the taxpayers, make up the difference. Still, the FDIC is a decent bargain. It's a backstop to panics—bank run panics anyway!) As long as banks make prudent loans, which, as we've seen in 2008, is not the greatest assumption.

Twin bargains. Twin safety nets for fractional reserve banking so we don't have to go back to the stifling days of gold. The Federal Reserve allows banks to post assets in exchange for loans to redeem depositors, in effect making the Fed the lender of last resort to banks. And then there's the FDIC, basically an insurance policy (up to $100,000 and sometimes $250,000) against bank runs, no matter how bad the bankers are at making loans. And who said banks are private companies?

All of this still means the Federal Reserve has to figure out exactly how much money to create to fill the bucket representing population growth and productivity—an almost impossible task.

The Fed has few levers. Interest rates are sometimes used in order to try to create just the right amount of money, with the Fed looking at prices—consumer prices and producer prices—as a surrogate for the price level. Prices are everything. Even though lower costs of computers and cell phones and LCD TVs is a positive for the economy and a wealth creator as the productive uses of technology always create wealth, it is often interpreted as deflationary, or at least *dis*inflationary, and perhaps as our techno-toys get cheaper, interest rates are cut to "stimulate" the economy.

Sometimes, when too much money is created, it doesn't show

up in consumer or producer prices, but flows into the stock market, or housing, and it appears to everyone as new wealth. Sometimes it is, but often stocks overshoot from excess money (see early 2000 and late 2007). But the run-up in house prices was worse, as houses are a first or maybe second derivative of wealth. Incomes go up from real wealth and some of that money goes into housing. But housing is often a false signal; too much money, especially leveraged, can increase housing beyond what wealth created. Same for commercial real estate, office buildings, and the like. It's a derivative of real wealth creation.

After the collapse of the banking system in the fall of 2008, hoarding became the order of the day. The world rushed into U.S. Treasuries. Short-term rates are almost zero. In the panic, the dollar became a safe harbor, jumping against the euro and the yen. No one wanted to spend money on houses, on cars, or even, gasp, on big-screen TVs. So the velocity of money shrank. To what? Well, no one really knows.

So to make up for lower velocity, to keep the economy from shrinking like a raisin, Fed chairman Ben Bernanke began increasing the monetary base to increase the amount of money. But it's hard. Even with bailout funds, banks didn't want to lend, so their 10:1 increase of Fed money didn't happen—let alone the 50:1 Bear Stearns money creation. So Bernanke started buying U.S. Treasuries, with cash, to increase the money supply. Which is pretty funny since he is also selling U.S. Treasuries to fund stimuli and budget deficits and . . .

Hey, wait a second, can't he just print $10 trillion and retire all the U.S. Treasury debt?

Uh, yeah, sure. Why not $100 trillion so we'll all be disgustingly rich? But print all you want; without productivity, there is no new wealth. The only real wealth is wealth that is created through productivity. The rest is just paper. Prices would go up to seek their new level to match all the extra money lying around. Two dollars for coffee at Starbucks would turn into twenty dollars. Big whoop, no one's any wealthier.

So PRINTING MONEY can't create wealth, but is it really just productivity? How about efficiency? Doesn't efficiency create wealth? Not long ago, I was asked to look at a company that had a cool way to increase the efficiency of internal combustion engines. I passed. "But it can save a billion barrels of oil every year," I was told. Uh-huh. Maybe. I've learned to avoid things that are efficient.

The words *productivity* and *efficiency* are often used interchangeably. Don't fall for it. They are related, but there are crucial differences. It's best to define productivity right now.

One way to look at it is like this: efficiency is about inputs while productivity is about outputs. Or maybe something like this: input/efficiency is the amount of effort put in while output/productivity is how much of something is produced and how often.

But even that's a bit too simple. Here is a better way of looking at it. To really understand all this, we need to add another word. Effectiveness is how outputs compare with what was planned or desired—doing the right things, while efficiency is the ratio of the amount of actual outputs to actual inputs—doing things right.

Productivity is really just doing the right things while doing things right. In other words, productivity is more or less the sum of effectiveness (doing the right things) and efficiency (doing things right).

That's a bit more fuzzy than productivity as output per worker hour, but it sure homes in on making sure you are going about generating outputs in ways that create wealth.

Think about it. You can have very efficient pyramid builders doing things the right way while being totally ineffective because they're not doing the right things—who needs pyramids?—there is no increase in wealth. A company that efficiently manufactures buggy whips or vacuum tubes is not creating wealth. Close to zero effectiveness.

Leonardo da Vinci famously designed and maybe even tried to build a helicopter in the fifteenth century. Highly effective, not very efficient.

My best advice when you hear the words *efficient* and *efficiency* is to turn around and run away as fast as you can.

Sure, you can squeeze 10 percent efficiency out of gas engines and save some money, but so what? It won't create much wealth. And certainly not wealth over decades.

Efficiency is a by-product—the world may get excited about it, but efficiency should never be the goal of a Free Radical. Google searches made looking stuff up extremely efficient, since you don't have to drive to the library, but that's secondary to the business of connecting advertisers and users, which is "the right thing to do" in addition to being a case of "doing things right."

INSTEAD OF SCALE, the word that most often gets thrown around is *sustainability*. Sustainable growth. Sustainable development, sustainable cities, sustainable architecture. But it's unclear what this even means—kind of an antiwaste thing. Thinking about sustainability, I decided it was time to get back in touch with George Gilder, so I fired off an e-mail:

gg,

where are you? any time to chat?

ajk

Andy,

Nice to hear from you. I miss the scarce Bordeaux. I'm in China, talking about the pending exaflood. Can we chat by email?

George

gg,

nice. email it is. ok, here it goes.

you can't swing a cat these days without hitting the world "sustainable." we can't overuse our planet's scarce resources, blah, blah. So what do you think about the word sustainable? doesn't it just mean that the new abundance hasn't been identified yet? does sustainable really mean "no growth"? that we're just throwing in the towel on progress?

ajk

Andy,

You see it every time. Appeals for sustainability always come at the end of the last cycle of abundance.

Don't be fooled. It's the vampire cycle, when the final blood is sucked out of markets that are dying. It's cash for clunkers and caps for energy production.

It's the ecological phase, when the impact of industries on the environment is judged more significant than their impact on human wealth and progress. It judges human beings as sources of CO_2 rather than of profitable new ideas and industries. It's the phase

of diminishing returns and administered socialism replacing the cycles of increasing returns of capitalist
enterprise.

It's the phase of new scarcities choking off the canonical abundances of the era. But it's always from
the darkest desperation from these scarcities that the
next era's abundance emerges as a savior. Wealth
gravitates to those that find it first or, better yet, make
it happen.

George

gg,

OK, I get that. so what do you do when confronted
with sustain-o-babble?

any clues to finding what's next?

ajk

Andy

"Sustain-o-babble" defines the prices that entrepreneurs have to beat with the new system, even
though the price is mind-share rather than economi-
cally definable. Why would anyone be attracted to a
business where prices are rising? It's a sign of obso-
letism. Think of it as a giant umbrella the next wave of
entrepreneurs can start pricing under and then lower
and lower their prices to begin the scaling process.
It's a gift.

George

gg,

a gift?

ajk

Andy,

Think about it. All the talk about scarcity of some soon-to-be-obsolete resource supplies profit signals galore for the suppliers of goods that bypass the sustainer's recycle bins. It implies large opportunities for transcending the recycles of sustainability with new cycles of abundance. Think outside the bin.

George

HE'S RIGHT. SUSTAINABILITY, or at least efficiency, is about doing things right, using fewer inputs. Fewer inputs? That doesn't sound wasteful. In other words, what you are making more efficient is no longer abundant, it's now become scarce. Yikes.

Efficient means you are at the end of a cycle, not the beginning. Something new, that scales, is almost by definition not efficient. You waste it. To hell with efficiency.

Rockefeller had a great run lowering the price of energy and changed how the world works, how many hours a day we can read, how far we can travel from our homes, and on and on. But when oil, which historically has always been wasted, starts to become scarce and we worry about how efficiently we can use it, what type of gas mileage our cars get, it's no longer the defining abundance of the era, is it?

Carnegie and Frick lowered the price of steel and we got cheaper buildings and railroads—until, of course, steel stopped getting cheaper. Vanderbilt lowered shipping and railroad costs by busting political entrepreneurs. But at some point, we reached the end of that cycle. Someone can make money at it—maybe a couple of Greek shipping magnates.

Think of a long declining cost curve. At some point, costs stop dropping. Efficiency is about getting the cost to drop again, by 10 percent or 15 percent, not the 90 percent or 99 percent that costs have already dropped to induce scale and the generation of wealth. When efficiency takes over, you are at the very end of this cycle. And efficiency is a one-off, not decades in duration.

Sustainability and efficiency are not for Free Radicals. Run away. When something's price goes up, it no longer Scales. It's no longer elastic. It's no fun anymore. Let everyone else worry about efficiency. It's so last-cycle.

Scale certainly helps you find things that are Productive. And make sure whatever it is Scales and is Productive over time. Will it be cheaper in three years, five years, a decade from now? Can you be the one to make it cheaper over time?

I KNOW THIS IS an aside, but I can't help noticing that the same economic forces like productivity that make horizontal companies rise in prominence have also driven the organization of the world economy into a horizontal enterprise. More than just software has gone horizontal or is driven by productivity!

China is still trying to bring a few 100 million or more people out of poverty. These are not highly educated or skilled workers. Not yet, anyway. They have to start doing menial tasks at low wages. When they are hired to assemble computer monitors and circuit boards, they can generate capital to increase living standards and educate succeeding generations to move up a layer. But in the meantime, they are not holding back other countries from rapid advances in technology.

Remember that the British and others went vertical and colonized large parts of the world to lock up natural resources to plug into their manufactories.

Both the Soviet Union and IBM, two raging, top-down, command-and-control systems, collapsed at about the same time.

No one denies that, as of 1989, the United States of America became the world's sole superpower. Our defense budget is more than that of the next ten countries combined. But so what? What are we going to do with it? Unlike past empires (Roman, British) or attempts (Soviets), there doesn't seem to be a huge desire by the United States to take over the rest of the world. Imperialism causes headaches. Only *Titanic/Avatar* movie director James Cameron wants to be King of the World. But we do preside over an empire of sorts, an empire created by the power of Silicon Valley and Wall Street. Gosh, that sounds evil, like a bad James Bond movie plot (one of those Timothy Dalton ones). But in reality, it ends up more benevolent than evil.

The United States versus the Soviet Union is the classic example of a productivity-producing horizontal enterprise and a resource-stealing vertical giant. Economies are about increasing the standard of living of their participants. If you don't have the economic system to create productivity, you end up stealing it from your neighbors. Hitler had a manufacturing engine, but felt Germans were above toiling in factories. So he chose to increase German living standards by the blitzkrieg process: take what you need by force. Grab territory. Steal their resources. Put them to work. Get rich.

The Soviets did the same thing. Expand, conquer, steal, rather than design, innovate, compete. And they lost to a nation that went the horizontal route. The United States bought manufactured goods from partners around the world, especially Japan and Germany. We could have made them stateside, owning them outright, but we didn't. It was better to let these countries run at their own pace, and own some horizontal layer (radios, clothes, cars).

The vertical Soviet system lost precisely because they had no productivity. If you just steal resources, there is no incentive for others to create productive solutions, to use abundance to make up for scarcity. In the end, capitalism out-wealthed socialism. We bankrupted them. They couldn't keep up. But my belief is that it was just as much the horizontal structure to our foreign policy and world trade that fueled capitalism's wealth creation.

What is America's place in the world? Are we imperialists? Nah. Are we philanthropists? Hardly. Are we greedy pigs, forcing the third world to toil in sweatshops for our benefit? Not really. Are we full of hubris and about to collapse under the weight of our own egos? Not a chance. Are we lowbrow double-wide-residing scum spreading our filthy culture around the world via TV reruns? Okay, this cultural thing has some merit, but it's not our fault. We don't force the Brazilians to watch *Baywatch* or the French to worship Jerry Lewis.

Globalization has linked the free world in a smart alliance. Computers, cell phones, and fiber optics are not made in any single country to be exported worldwide, but instead have components and labor from more than thirty tightly linked countries, including China and Vietnam.

The world economy transitioned from loosely knit but mainly stand-alone industrialized countries through the 1970s to a tightly wound digital ecosystem today. It's not so obvious yet, but I'm convinced that digital technology has rendered imperialism and territorialism obsolete. Why take over a country and deal with the headaches of a welfare system, and have to fix the plumbing in Uzbekistan, when you can buy their output on the cheap, even ordering their goods over the Web? Despite all the protests, globalization instills peace. Trade now represents 26 percent of world GDP, up from 18 percent in 1990.

Today, the United States has the ability to use its power in unique ways. Rather than being imperialists, we sit on top of a naturally organizing Horizontal Empire. Horizontal rules!

It turns out, much to the annoyance of Starbucks-trashing globalistas, that free markets and capitalism can run amok and create wonderful things. Is this some sort of capital Darwinism or, worse, a dog-eat-dog (and I'm wearing Milk Bone underwear) existence?

Yes, but it works. Without much forethought or planning or a dictator, benevolent or otherwise, the world has structured itself into a horizontal wealth-creating and peace-maintaining system— a productive system that actually increases the standard of living of all the participants, not just those in the United States. America still sits on top of the heap, sure, but wealth has increased for every country, company, or person that contributes. And they get rich not by stealing from the rest of the world, but by adding value to the food chain.

ALL INDUSTRIES WERE at one point productive, or they probably wouldn't exist. It was easier to print books with the Gutenberg press than to have monks write them out by hand. But the productivity gains, the pop in society's standard of living, only lasted for so long. Back then, maybe it lasted a century or two. But eventually everyone printed books and it was no longer a source of productivity gains. Electricity beat burning candles for added reading hours or burning wood for cooking and warmth.

Automobiles were a heck of a lot more productive than walking, to get you to work or to the store to buy a half-gallon of milk. But at some point, cars became safe, reliable, and ubiquitous. Cars also stopped improving, in the United States anyway (you're not getting there any faster), so they no longer provide productivity and increased wealth.

Vacuums and toasters and dishwashers are labor-saving devices, but they saved the labor a long time ago and no longer create productivity and wealth.

Movies were more productive than taking a Broadway show on the road from town to town to tell entertaining stories or sing sappy musicals. But not anymore.

Answering machines and voice mail increased productivity at work (and of course got rid of a whole pack of pink pad *While You Were Out* message transcribers, but more on that in another Rule). Today there are a billion voice mail boxes and some 40 billion voice mails left every year. Regardless of the fact that most messages are worthless, the productivity pop from voice mail is all in the past.

Think of productivity as a one-off thing, unless the source of productivity constantly improves. Free Radicals need a continuum of productivity gains to keep creating new wealth.

Adapt to Humans; Don't Make Them Adapt to You

THERE IS A LONG HISTORY OF PEOPLE ADAPTING TO TECH-nology. What a waste.

Free Radicals instead need to make technology that adapts to humans.

We learned to drive cars with a steering wheel, a gas pedal, and a brake pedal (and for those of us who like to have fun, a clutch pedal too). The basic car design doesn't appear to come from a series of human interaction studies or from polls or even from er-gonomic regulations. It was the design of the horseless carriage, which itself was adapted from the horse and carriage. It works. We adapt to it and learn how to drive. Railroads were laid in the ruts of horse-drawn wagons. My microwave oven kind of looks like my regular oven, but with more buttons.

The old Microsoft DOS command line interface looked just like that of Digital Equipment's PDP-11 minicomputers, which looked like that of the mainframes that preceded those.

But as technology Scales, more and more of its power is sucked into the task of interfacing with us stupid humans.

Often, technology is productive for early adopters who easily figure out how to use it, and then painfully unproductive for the next several hundred million people to jump onboard. This can last for years and years. But real success comes from hiding the technology from users.

Inventor (and my next-door neighbor) Doug Engelbart had a dream of human augmentation, and gave the ultimate demonstration at an Association of Computing Machinery meeting back in 1968, with menus and hypertext and his wooden three-button mouse. You can find the video online in scratchy black and white. Well worth the watch. His vision took decades to implement.

Windows icons and pull-down menus and mouse clicks were not only more intuitive than a command line prompt, they helped increase the productivity of users. But not right away. It seems every time a new technology comes out, we play with it for years until we can figure it out, and then we buy into the new interface and don't ever want to change, until the next new thing comes along, Vista or Google or the iPhone, which we fuss with for a few years and get our productivity humming again and swear this is it, this is all we need, we're never gonna change again.

iPods are pretty "plug and play" and hide the details about bit rate encoding and MP3 files from the masses. And texts and e-mails are pretty easy to send and receive. But there's still a lot to be done. Like what? Well, how about machines that speak in the language of humans—literally. Quit making us type. We speak, we listen, we move our hands around. We point. We smile. We pout. Use it all.

One of the ways that I spot the next cool thing is by tracking the video game business. They're often on the crest of the next wave of productivity. Game machines, both old arcade games and home video game consoles like the Commodore 64, had graphics and icons and trackballs well before mainstream PCs. The Nintendo Wii and the WiiMote clearly point the way to sensors tracking our movements as another input interface. Same with the iPhone, which features not only an accelerometer for motion sensing, but multitouch finger flicking gestures to change pages and zoom in and out.

Microsoft one upped the Nintendo Wii with Project Natal—what looks like a bar with three imaging sensors in it to create a three-dimensional camera. The camera can recognize gestures for games—tennis, boxing, whatever. But a Free Radical can almost see the application guys elsewhere at Microsoft drooling over the idea of incorporating gestures into everything they do. Looking at Project Natal, a Free Radical can smell a decade of advancement and cost declines and new uses never before possible. Image and face recognition? Why not? It's just code.

Voice interfaces are teed up as well. Put two microphones instead of one in PCs and cell phones, like the iPhone, and you can get rid of background noise and virtually point the microphones at a speaker to figure out exactly what is being said in the middle of a hurricane. Today's voice recognition is mostly awful, but that can be solved with not only faster and more powerful devices at the edge of the network but with algorithms and look-up tables to figure out spoken words and context, which will reside in the cloud.

The same is going to happen with biotech and personalized medicine. The biotech industry got big creating new drugs that address smaller and smaller markets, but more effectively. But now what?

Already there is a proliferation of protein tests and genomic tests that can start to figure out what unique disease and unique type of cancer you might have. The possibility of creating custom drugs is on the horizon, though held in check by Food and Drug Administration rules oriented around treating everyone with the same disease with the same drugs, rather than personalized one-off drugs. But remember, technology trumps policy. Once it exists, the regulators will adapt to the new reality.

I'd hate to be the first one through their hoops, but once a personalization window is open, billions of dollars will pass through it as millions of lives are extended. Tools to sequence genes can be harnessed to identify and locate disease, as well as customize treatment. Lying down in giant imagers in specialized hospital rooms will give way to using handheld imagers. Beyond entertainment, this is what anyone with wealth beyond food and shelter spends their dough on. And gladly, if it keeps them ticking.

OKAY, AS MUCH as I'm intrigued by personalized technology and personalized medicine, that's not what I'm *really* talking about. Those things are in the physical realm. All great stuff, all with enormous productivity possibilities and huge upsides and big pots of wealth in their future.

But true adaptive technologies are things that adapt to how you think. This is the big change over the next two decades. This is what a Free Radical will want to harness.

Figure out what people want. What song they want to hear next as the Pandora music service does, what menu they will click on next, which search results are most pertinent. Since the dawn of computers, there have been efforts at so-called artificial intelligence. None of it has amounted to much. IBM mainframes are being trained to play (and win) *Jeopardy!* It's a start.

But I think the time is right for machines to adapt. Again, all those powerful machines at the edge and huge networks of servers in the cloud with giant repositories of all the things we've done, what our friends are doing, what the average twenty-seven-year-old from Sheboygan, Wisconsin, is likely to do.

Amazon uses a limited version of this in their recommendations, but more as a marketing tool to get you to buy yet another book. Others who view this item bought this book. We recommend that. They look for patterns and crudely overlay them on your page views in their system. Netflix, the DVD rental and streaming video company, offered a prize of $1 million for a better algorithm to suggest movies you might like to watch. These are all early adopters of the adaptive model.

But why not recommend books based on my search history? If I'm searching on Google for information on the Ottoman Empire, surely there are a dozen books that ought to pop up that will be of interest immediately, without me heading to Amazon to find out. Now that is adaptive. Heck, you ought to be able to tell me what my next three searches are going to be. Think one move ahead. That's adaptive.

Or show me what shows I ought to be watching, based on what I've already watched, what my friends are watching, what's being talked about in blogs I read, what's being talked about in blogs in general, what shows are coming up on the Ottoman Empire and on and on. I can search for this stuff myself, but who has time, or the attention span? As Doug Engelbart points out, augment me. Tell me what restaurants to go to, what articles to read, what fashion to overpay for and on and on.

This is not easy stuff to pull off. Riches will be heaped on Free Radicals who solve the adaptive puzzle, because at the end of the day, augmentation is the ultimate in productivity and we will all benefit. It's not without its thorns—privacy being the biggest one—but it's going to be as big a game-changer as everything else. If you can harness adaptive technology, so many other things will fall into place.

By the way, voice recognition and personalized medicine have both been spectacular failures as businesses. Am I wrong about this adaptive thing? I don't think so—there is always the risk of being too early. You don't front-run Abundance or Scale or what can happen at the edge. Timing is the trickiest part of using these Rules. Something may sound good and still be way too early. I really think that figuring out where technology is along that cost curve will both keep Free Radicals out of trouble and provide conviction when the time is right.

Be Soylent—Eat People

Now that machines are adapting to humans, it's time to think more and more about us humanoids: what we do, what kinds of jobs we have, and how society can best utilize living, breathing humans to increase standards of living. I've spent a lot of time thinking about this, and my conclusion: the best way to leverage Abundance and Scale and to create Productivity is to get rid of people.

There, I said it. Don't hate me; I'm just the messenger.

Now I'm not suggesting we actually eat anyone, as in the 1973 Charlton Heston sci-fi cult classic, *Soylent Green*, about overpopulation in the year 2022 ("Soylent Green is people!"). But we do need to get rid of worthless jobs. On the surface, I know that this might sound contrary to the old "help your fellow man" mantra, but really, truly, the road to wealth passes through the graveyard of today's jobs.

Adam Smith figured this out a long time ago. In *The Wealth of Nations*, he wrote that "all useful machines and instruments of trade" were designed to "facilitate and abridge labour." Reduce. Condense. Curtail. Swim with the fishes.

But which ones?

The English classification system was quite simple:

Tinker, Tailor, Soldier, Sailor

Rich Man, Poor Man, Beggar Man, Thief

And then Americans added: Doctor, Lawyer, Indian Chief.

Probably a good place to start!

MY OLDEST SON, Kyle, got a summer job at a biotech newsletter company in Silicon Valley. All documents that arrived at the company were scanned and saved as PDF files. The company paid high school and college interns ten dollars an hour to open the files, read a few lines to figure out what was inside them, and then re-name them for later reference. Pretty dull stuff, but it beat digging ditches, my son told me. He would listen to music, read his e-mail, send texts, update his Facebook status, anything to pass the time.

Hearing this, I suggested that someone (my son perhaps . . . hint, hint) write a piece of code to automatically rename the files based on a simple set of rules. Dripping with sarcasm, he shot back, "Do you know how many people wouldn't have summer jobs if you did that?"

But that's the point, isn't it? There is nothing productive about these kinds of jobs, though they are necessary for this company, and many companies, until someone, a true Free Radical, writes a piece of code to make them obsolete. That's how you create productivity.

I stayed at the lovely Hotel Lombardy on my last trip to Washington, D.C. I pushed the elevator button to head up to my room, heard a buzzing and was shocked when a uniformed elevator operator opened the door and asked which floor I was headed to. And yes, it was an Otis elevator. Talk about waste (the bad kind).

Think of how many elevator operators have been put out of work over time, all because of some nifty transistors and relays and, now, some clever code. Think of how many security guards have been put out of work by cheap cameras and disk drives for storing surveillance video. All in the name of progress.

Okay, these are pretty obvious examples. But across the economy, the real task is to figure out which jobs going forward need to be eaten. That's where you find the opportunity for upside and wealth.

IN HIS 1906 play *The Doctor's Dilemma*, George Bernard Shaw wrote that "all professions are conspiracies against the laity," or lay people, common folk. I hate quoting dead playwrights almost as much as quoting dead economists, but at least there are plenty of live writers coming up with good stuff every day. As a member of the Fabian Society (a precursor to Britain's Labour Party), Shaw spoke often about income equality and an equitable division of land and capital. But in a strange way, he makes the point for progress, by looking suspiciously at every profession for conspiracies against you and me.

If you look at the world through a productivity filter, a lot more things start to make sense, especially about who is pulling their load and who is just along for the ride. So here is my attempt.

I've always been a fan of dividing the world into different types of people. As a wise person once said, "There are two types of people in the world: those that divide the world into two types of people and those that don't." I'm a divider.

George Bernard Shaw also said that "the secret to success is to offend the greatest number of people." So here I go.

There are actually two types of people in the world—Creators and Servers.

CREATORS ARE AT the top of the food chain—those who create productivity.

The Makes versus the Takes. The Vital Few. I don't care if they are doing it themselves or work at a company that does. Productivity is precious—we need to take it wherever we can get it. Someone is creating tools from what is abundant to make up for what is scarce.

Some create abundance, while others figure out how to put that abundance to use. There are different types of Creators.

A Creator might be someone writing a piece of code to automatically lay out magazines, getting rid of expensive graphic designers. Or designing a robot to pick and place a product into an Amazon box for shipping, getting rid of workers in a warehouse. Or writing algorithms for trading stocks in milliseconds, something humans couldn't do even if you threw a thousand of them at the problem.

Or maybe a Creator has come up with a drug that lowers the risk of some debilitating disease. Or a test to identify cancer five years early. A Creator can increase output by saving lives and keeping people healthy, too.

One might even create a better system for stocking shelves. Yes, sometimes Creators do the same thing that tons of other people are already doing, but they do it an order of magnitude better. Wal-Mart automated their purchasing and distribution systems (thanks to some awesome Creators) so they could sell the same goods as local stores for much cheaper. Although it is vilified by local merchants, enough local residents have voted with their wallets by paying less for the same stuff to make Wal-Mart one of the world's most profitable companies. Soon copied by Home Depot, Costco, and Best Buy.

In fact, since around 1991, aided by the variously timed downfalls of Ames and Carter Hawley Hale and Allied Stores, retail productivity has been on a hot streak. More output with fewer people. After bouncing between +3 percent and -3 percent productivity between 1974 and 1991, retail has been rising, hitting a peak of 5 percent around 2005, outpacing the gains of the technology sector.

The profits generated by Creators are the true wealth of society. They do something useful for the world better and usually cheaper than it could be done before. The founders and the shareholders of the Creator companies make handsome profits, as they should, and the stock market showers them with wealth. Well-deserved wealth. Why? Because whoever paid for the products or services offered by the Creator did it by choice, because it was cheaper or better than any of the alternatives. If I pay $5 for a two-by-four at my local lumber yard versus $3 at Home Depot, I am not only wasting $2 (I might as well burn two George Washingtons), I am encouraging the local lumber yard to keep doing what they are doing, overcharging and then not reinvesting their profits into a more productive system that would make their price competitive. In effect, I'm doing a disservice to society by overpaying. How dumb is that?

All the examples I've given so far of Scale and Intelligence at the Edge and Horizontals are at heart about Creators.

Creators are usually designers of productive things. But they can also be manufacturers, if they can do it better. And they can be services, if they run their service better and cheaper than others can. Think online airline ticketing, banking, or music distribution.

WITH THE ALL-IMPORTANT Creators out of the way, the question becomes, who do you get rid of? If the idea is to get rid of people to increase productivity, which ones? And should you feel guilty?

As far as guilt, forget about it. Buggy whip manufacturers are out of business. So are pyramid designers. And, for the most part, sheet music printers. Good riddance.

The trick is to identify those who stand in the way of increased output. Who provides a service that is best done with fewer people? The obvious ones like bank tellers and travel agents and long-distance operators have already mostly been eaten. Let's dig into what different types of workers do. Then we'll eat the ones in our way. And lose the guilt. Not only do we have huge safety nets, but they'll be rehired soon enough. Don't let anecdotes of despair bring you down. There's a Say's law for employment too: Over time, employment grows to fill the economy. In other words, in the long run, better jobs are created that more than make up for those that are destroyed.

I LABEL EVERYONE WHO is not a Creator a Server. But even that is too broad a definition. Generically, Servers are the next tier down—those who provide service to the Creators. Creators can't do it all by themselves. They have to eat, put their money somewhere, get haircuts, get their teeth fixed, forge contracts, and on and on. This requires legions of Servers setting up shop all over the place to take care of others. Society has built an entire service sector just to service the Creators, and, well, all the other Servers.

Often, Servers make decent money, enough to be part of the middle class. They are doing their part. Not knocking the ball out of the park, but not flipping burgers either. Servers earn all levels of pay, more or less in line with the value of the service they provide. Cashiers and baggers at the low end, followed by receptionists and furniture movers and painters, then plumbers and carpenters, then graphic artists and marketers, all the way to lawyers and doctors.

Shoeshine boy, paper delivery, I can go on and on. None of these create any wealth, because they aren't creating any productivity, that is, more output per worker hour. But if a clever shoeshine boy tied shoe brushes to a broomstick handle so he could shine six pairs of shoes at once, I'd happily bump him up to the rank of Creator.

The same is true of home builders. Homes are consumptive, not productive. A Take versus a Make. If you create better building materials or can build a neighborhood in an assembly line, then maybe you've got something productive. If not, you're just milking Creators.

The vast majority of workers are Servers. They don't know it, and probably wouldn't like being called that, but they are. Thank them for existing, as they do buy Creators' stuff, but they are not Creators.

Sloppers are one mutation of Servers. It is too broad to label everyone as merely a Server. Sure, plenty of people make stuff, and a lot of it is made productively (using Creator-made tools, of course), creating wealth. But there are legions that do nothing but move stuff from one side of things to another—across a factory floor, a warehouse, across town, or across the economy. They're not Creators—just middlemen or brokers, marking up the price for slopping stuff around—milking someone else's inventions and adding cost.

I call them Sloppers because they're just slopping stuff around without adding any real value. You can argue, perhaps, that by getting the right goods to the right place at the right time to make a sale, they are adding value. Maybe. Especially as more and more of output is services that can move at the speed of light down fiber strands. But they are still middlemen. Value? Not much.

A friend who works at a large multinational Japanese consumer electronics firm was pushing to increase productivity by putting in new systems that would make entire departments of people obsolete. "Before we invest in that automation you're asking for," the higher-ups said, "we'll need the employee IDs of the people and jobs we'd be eliminating." Can you imagine the politics once that list of employees appeared at a staff meeting?

Longshoremen are the ultimate Sloppers, moving things from ship to shore and back again. San Francisco used to be a vibrant port, with piers built on the Embarcadero along the edge of the city. But in 1971, the International Longshoremen's and Warehousemen's Union (ILWU) went on strike for 106 days to fight against container ships. Containerization had become all the rage in shipping. With huge cranes, you load a ship up with containers, which can be unloaded at the other end and hooked to tractor trailer trucks and driven to their final destination. No need for dock workers to unload ships box by box, by hand, with a few boxes inevitably ending up damaged, up to some threshold of "breakage," pushed to the side as "bonuses" for the workers. The ILWU didn't like the idea of unloading a ship in fifteen hours instead of over several days, and without a huge army of union-wage workers. The ILWU fought against "steady men," crane operators hired directly rather than through the union. The ILWU eventually lost the strike and all the shipping business moved from San Francisco to Oakland across the Bay.

You'd think lessons would have been learned.

In 2002, I attended a baseball game in San Francisco's Pac Bell Park, now AT&T Park. Looking out over the Bay, it was hard not to notice dozens and dozens of huge container ships, piled high and sitting low in the water. This time, the ILWU had gone on strike to protect the jobs of marine clerks, union workers at every gate who, armed with pen and clipboard, tracked container ships coming and going and handed out orders on paper slips to truckers telling them which container they were to pick up. What was the ILWU so worried about this time? Bar code readers and wireless technology and computers to track the containers as well as an ATM-like machine to provide truckers with their orders. Classic people-eating technology.

Technology eats people. Someone inevitably complains, but progress cannot be fought for long. Creating wealth means finding those jobs to eat.

Add to the mix of people all the overhead in getting something to market. All the government workers at the Department of Commerce, the Department of Energy, Department of Education, the Federal Trade Commission, and on and on. Buildings full of people who don't add much if any real value or help create productive wealth; they often just burden the system with costs. Don't mistake them for plain old Servers as they don't provide any useful service, just a cost. Sure, you gotta have them up to a point, but in no way are they increasing output or adding anything to the productivity stock of society.

Government employees are a unique bunch and almost all are

Sloppers. I was fortunate to have a conversation with author P. J. O'Rourke. And not just author (I've read all his books, *Holidays in Hell* and *Eat the Rich*, they're all terrific), no, P.J. always gets the additional modifier of "satirist." How cool is that? O'Rourke has an eagle eye for how society really works and calls it like he sees it, with humor. It's not really satire at all; it's telling the truth, which can be even funnier. P.J. and I chatted about his book on cars, *Driving Like Crazy*, when I asked him about all the rules and regulations and government workers that bog down the automakers.

"You mean the Fun Suckers?" he asked.

"I guess . . ."

"Think about the kid-has-to-put-a-hockey-helmet-on-to-answer-the-phone society we live in now," he said. "These Fun Suckers are very interesting and they have been around forever and they are certainly not limited to any one political party or one political point of view. But they do gravitate towards politics and they are the people who come and tell you that everything you do is bad for you, bad for other people, insensitive, divisive, harms the climate, is unsustainable, it leaves too large a carbon footprint, it tangles things in the tuna nets that shouldn't be tangled in them. Everything you do, wrong colored bathing suit destroys the manta ray population. Whatever. They've always got some reason to tell you what to do."

"Again and again." I added.

"Of course," P.J. continued, "and if you really think about it, it's just a form of bullying for weaklings. These are not the kind of people that got to do a lot of bullying on the school yard. In fact, they probably got beat up a lot. But now that they've reached the fullness of age and maturity, they've figured out a way to bully us ordinary people. And it's always something to be analyzed."

"But why?" I wanted to know.

"Politics is the art of achieving power and prestige without merit."

Government employees are classic Sloppers. Necessary? Sure, to some extent, but for the most part, these Sloppers are wealth destroyers, not Creators or adding much value to anything.

I WASN'T SURE WHERE to put marketers. Let's call them **Super Sloppers**. You know the type. They take a $5 sneaker, put Michael Jordan's name on it, run expensive commercials, and then turn around and sell it for $150. Quite the parlor trick. Marketing and branding create value out of nothing. It's all in your mind. They're playing with your psyche.

I'm as guilty as everyone else for falling for this scam, and I feel like a moron whenever I overpay for something, from cars to T-shirts to watches. There is no economic value, no productivity, gained from a shirt sporting an Adidas logo, which I just noticed I'm wearing right now. What a moron I am! I pay them to be a walking billboard for them.

A $10 digital Casio watch, let alone the clock on your cell phone synced with an atomic clock, keeps better time than a Patek Philippe wind-up with fourteen jewels, whatever jewels have to do with keeping time.

Super Sloppers aren't moving stuff from one side of a warehouse to another—more like moving stuff from the generic side of your mind to the "luxurious, won't people think I'm awesome, we descended from peacocks" side of the brain.

A Burberry scarf. Oakley sunglasses. Jimmy Choo shoes. The markups on these things are amazing. If people want to pay, that's their deal. But this stuff is not real wealth, just the impression of wealth, perceived wealth. Or better, the spoils of wealth.

Organic food is a wonderful Super Slopper invention. It uses fewer chemicals, so it should cost less, right? Not a chance. Better for your health? Doubtful. Better for the environment? Maybe, but at what cost to consumers? How much are you paying for the value of organic food, or is it just a perceived value because you "feel" better? I love walking through Whole Foods and asking where the free-range strawberries are. Look, I don't care if you spend the money on this stuff—just realize that you're the sucker, not me, except when it comes to Adidas shirts! Same with fashion. I'm not suggesting we should all dress in Maoist shirts with too-long sleeves, but don't try to convince me that what the wealthy buy has anything to do with creating wealth.

Much of the eco-enviro movement is Super Slopping. And of course, hybrid cars. The Toyota Prius is an expensive status symbol that says you care about the planet, with a price tag a good 30 percent more than a regular car with similar gas mileage.

I asked (satirist) P. J. O'Rourke if he would ever drive a Prius.

"No," he said a little too quickly and the laughed. "I wouldn't, though not that there is anything wrong with an electric car or hybrid. Teslas are a hot dog of a car. Hybrid is an interesting technology, big locomotives dragging giant freight trains are just hybrids. No, I don't mind the technology, what I mind is the smugness. Prius is a smug mobile. 'Oh, I am smug, I am saving the planet, I'm so good.' I can't stand it. So, if you have a loud Prius, or maybe if you're driving it topless, or if you drive it in a dangerous way, then I'm okay. Which would be hard to do because they're so slow."

Not much later, I had Sunday lunch with billionaire Johann Rupert and my friend Rob Hersov at an Italian restaurant in London. Johann runs Richemont, the Swiss luxury goods company that owns Cartier and Mont Blanc and Dunhill, among others. It is a fantastic business, with great operating margins and cash flow. We started talking about technology and Johann was complaining about the iPhone, that it was pretty much a toy and overpriced compared to his old Nokia phone that ran for almost a week without needing a charge.

Now, I happened to agree, but I tried to explain that not only does it do a few things that other phones can't, like helping me find the right Underground station to get to this restaurant, but that it also had this amazing effect on people who felt like they were at the leading edge by using it, that they were somehow different from and cooler than everyone else (never mind the tens of millions that have been sold). That whole smug thing that P. J. O'Rourke talked about. But in this case, it was part productive and part pretty. And of all people to understand this, it should have been Johann Rupert. (Actually, I'm sure he did, but he was understandably pissed that someone else was weaseling in on his game.)

What I didn't say was that the iPhone was basically $500 versus the $50,000 watch Johann was wearing to tell him what day it was and the phase of the moon.

Actually, his watch makes him one of the ultimate Super Sloppers. I was going to ask him for it, but dessert was served and the conversation flipped to the mess that private equity and investment banks created, which reminds me that at some point I have to put financial types into one of these categories.

SPONGES ARE NEXT. Compensation of many Servers and even Sloppers can be quite skewed, leaving a false impression of their value. Sponges are the ones who employ several little tricks to increase their pay without their really adding value, like real estate brokers or lawyers who would be just ordinary Servers but instead are highly paid, sponging off the rest of us.

One annoying trick to create Sponges is to limit the supply of workers to decrease competition and most likely increase prices and pay above and beyond their true economic value. By limiting supply, you can have Servers who are overcompensated. And how do they do that? Via some bogus licensing requirement. Jeff Rowes, an attorney at the Institute for Justice in Arlington, Virginia, wrote in *The Wall Street Journal* that "America has become a patchwork quilt of laws serving special interests because courts refuse to protect economic liberty. In 1950, only one in twenty trades required a license. Now it is more than one in four . . . and the clamor by industry groups for more licensing grows unabated. Special interests love licensing because it restricts competition and thus drives up the prices they can charge. None of this would be possible if judges simply struck down licensing laws as an insult to the constitutional right to earn an honest living secured by the due process clause of the Fifth Amendment and the 'privileges or immunities' clause of the Fourteenth Amendment."

Want to cut hair? No problem, you just need to pass a beautician exam so you can get a beautician's license to cut hair. Then you can charge $25 for a fifteen-minute men's haircut. Kind of ridiculous. Even more for a shampoo and rinse that I'm pretty good at doing myself at home.

Real estate agents need a real estate license. Stock brokers need to pass a Series 7 and other nonsensical tests before they can enter stock trades. Oddly, real people like you and me don't need the same license to make trades on E*Trade.

Plumbers need licenses, and so do electricians. Turns out, so does the tree guy who cut up a giant oak tree that fell in my yard and charged me $120 an hour on a Sunday and then $80 an hour on Monday and Tuesday. I told him that I didn't hire a lawyer to cut up the tree.

And yes, lawyers are the most blatant at this. States require lawyers to pass a local bar exam, under the premise that we only want smart lawyers practicing in our state. But really, it's about limiting supply. A good lawyer is worth every penny and we all should be free to pay up to access great advice. But so much of what lawyers do is rote and repetitive, especially the discovery process in lawsuits, yet firms still charge well above economic value for these types of services, turning Servers into Sponges. The hottest area for corporate general counsels is electronic discovery, or e-discovery. A Free Radical product that gets rid of Sponges! Use computers to scan documents for keywords and potentially incriminating evidence rather than pay law firms huge fees to have paralegals read millions of dull and boring documents, and still likely miss the juicy stuff.

Another all-time-favorite game is to organize workers into unions and demand higher pay. I don't want to go into this too much, as unions have been on the decline—a third of U.S. workers were in unions in 1950, 20 percent in 1983, and maybe 12 percent today—and they often are parasites that kill the mother ship via unproductive work rules that lower output per worker. I'll talk about this more in another Rule.

Think of highly paid union workers as Sponges, extracting pay above and beyond their economic value because of laws passed under the guise of protecting workers, when in reality it's just an economic shakedown. Sadly, it just means Creators have to create even more to make up for this inefficiency in the system for those that are, you guessed it, destroying wealth. I appreciate some of the value of unions in stopping corporations from exploiting workers (unsafe conditions, threats of termination), but once again, the compensation they extract is often well above the value of the workers, hence the label of Sponges.

And what about doctors? They need to pass a medical exam to practice medicine. Sponges, right? Not quite. More on that below.

Oh and by the way, don't confuse Sponges with **Slackers**. They are a different beast. Unlike Sponges, Slackers are easy to spot: white guys with dreadlocks, people who hang around Starbucks, women in long dresses made out of old drapes. Sponges are hard but not impossible to get rid of. The more they charge, the easier it is to find them and get rid of them, via e-discovery or things like it. For those that we are stuck with, a little competition ought to do the trick to turn them back into ordinary Servers.

Slackers don't do anything, so you can't get rid of them. It's why I won't bother to describe them further, except to say that without Creators creating productive wealth, Slackers would be hard at work shoveling manure onto free-range strawberries.

THERE IS AN entirely separate set of Sponges who masquerade as entrepreneurs and sometimes even try to pass themselves off as Creators. Don't be fooled—peel away the mask and you'll find **Thieves**, political entrepreneurs who rob society blind (no peeking, but there's more on this in a later Rule).

Want an example? Start with cell phone operators. They "own" radio spectrum, an exclusive license from the Federal Communications Commission. They were either handed the spectrum during the early days of the industry, or bought it at auction over the last fifteen years. By buying it, they put on pretenses that they were really entrepreneurs, buying an input (a medium, a conduit, a pipe) and then applying capital, labor, and technology to it and creating a service to society that increases productivity. But it's a false pretense. They just pass along the cost of the auction to consumers. We all vastly overpay for cell phone service because these guys have exclusive licenses. Sure, there is AT&T and Verizon and Sprint and, in a smaller way, T-Mobile, but notice that none of them compete on price. They come up with incomprehensible per-minute service plans that have nothing to do with their costs.

Yes, there is productivity—I can talk in the car instead of pulling over and using a pay phone (do those even exist anymore?). But there is very little relation between the price I pay and their costs in providing this value to me. I am paying a tax to these guys because they have an exclusive license to the spectrum. It's a government-mandated supply constraint.

Same for cable TV. Comcast and Time Warner Cable have, for the most part, exclusive rights town by town to run cable and offer cable TV services. It's supposed to be competition but it rarely is. Worse, they raise prices every year above and beyond the inflation rate, because, well, because they can. It's another tax based on a government-guaranteed monopoly. They are economic Thieves. They are destroying wealth by making all of us overpay for their services—money that could have been spent on something productive that created wealth rather than spiking it.

Broadcasters own valuable TV spectrum, and for the longest time there were only three broadcast networks, ABC, CBS, and NBC, with a set of arcane laws protecting their government-mandated franchises. Then the laws were amended to allow for a fourth network, Fox.

And this leaks to other markets. Because of high advertising rates, broadcasters overpay for the Super Bowl, the NBA Finals, the World Series, and the Masters. The NFL passes along these fees to owners who, through collective bargaining, are forced to pass them along to players. No one is worth $10 million a year to catch a football like Terrell Owens, or $25 million a year to play shortstop and hit like Derek Jeter. (Yes, they are part of the "vital few," but vital to our entertainment, not wealth creation!)

Because of the exclusivity of media, Heineken (a Super Slopper) pays up and then passes along their advertising costs in the form of higher beer prices. So does General Motors. And Nike. You and I pay Derek Jeter, not the New York Yankees–owning Steinbrenners. Not that I blame athletes for milking the Creators. If I could hit .300, I would too. Athletes may be indirect Thieves, but Thieves nonetheless. Their profit is your loss.

ESPN charges some $2.50 per month per subscriber, because Comcast offers it on their basic tier. You pay whether you watch or not. They turn around and overpay for sporting events. The owners overpay players, and on and on. I love to watch sports, but this system of false scarcity is a tax on me, a tax on my stupidity. I am being robbed. You may be too!

Other political Thieves? Well, banks. In exchange for accepting regulation, they can borrow money from the Federal Reserve and turn around and lend it to us at much higher rates. Seen your credit card bill after accidentally forgetting to pay right on time? Tony Soprano would blush.

Electric utilities are government-mandated Thieves.

Insurance companies are heavily regulated, creating a false scarcity and higher rates.

What about public school teachers? 'Fraid so. They are government-mandated and have a strong union that fights against anything productive, from merit pay to changes in class size. Plus, it's practically impossible to fire them no matter how incompetent, and as any parent knows there are some good teachers and a whole bunch who are just making it in. A 2009 study by SRI International, paid for by the Education Department, concluded that "on average, students in online learning conditions performed better than those receiving face-to-face instruction." Hmm. Look, these are mostly honest people in a business that is politically corrupt. They are generically Thieves, as I've defined it, even if they are individually perfectly honest and responsible citizens. But whether they recognize it or not, they are still milking the system and therefore have jobs that might be able to be eliminated to increase the wealth of the rest of society. Of course further studies need to be done to determine if online learning truly is effective. If it is, we should at least begin the discussion on restructuring education and utilizing similar productivity tools and techniques that work in the rest of the economy.

Others? Car dealers have local monopolies. So do hospitals.

And doctors? They limit the number of medical schools, and require students to pass a medical exam. But that only gets them halfway there. They still somehow need to overcharge. A Dartmouth College study suggests that $700 million of the $2 trillion that the United States spends on health care every year is wasted on unnecessary or unwanted procedures. There, doctors are in cahoots with lawyers.

A 2009 letter to the editor in *The Wall Street Journal* by Dr. Jerry McKnight sums it up best: "I estimate in my practice that 20% of the tests, studies, imaging procedures, medicines, and referrals are not needed, but are ordered in order to attempt to prevent litigation. In my private talks with other physicians they have indicated that this is consistent with their experience."

Conservatively, doctors make at least 20 percent more than they should. Classic economic Thieves, no matter what the rationale, and there is always some bogus rationale. Cell phone companies insist they need to charge huge rates to pay for more towers and infrastructure, when it should be the opposite—they pay for their system and then profit by offering it at competitive rates.

Look, we need all these things, from phones to lawyers to doctors, and yes, even high-definition broadcasts of the NCAA Final Four. But don't believe for a second that anyone delivering that service is creating real wealth. They are destroying wealth by stealing their fees above and beyond their worth. Unlike marketers, who play with our minds, Thieves usually hide behind some piece of legislation. There is a difference. I'd rather have the choice.

Thieves are usually easy to find. If a signature on a law ending exclusivity were to pass, would they generate the profits they do? If the answer is no, then you've found your Thief! Fortunately, technology can de facto rip up these exclusivity deals well before lawmakers act.

I WASN'T SURE WHAT to do about people in finance—bankers, brokers, traders, venture capitalists, hedge fund managers, folks in private equity? I'd love to lump all of Wall Street into one neat bundle and call them Thieves—"those greedy bastards who caused the markets to melt down," right?——but I can't. Of course, I was one of them for way too many years, and I have a soft spot for Wall Street, but my biases are in check. Why? Because innovators and entrepreneurs need capital. And capital is hard to come by. People with money don't just trust any knucklehead who walks down the street, hand him money, and tell him to just make it grow. And even the greatest idea needs capital to get it going: McDonald's,

Kraft's Cheez Whiz, or Intel's 1103 1-kilobit dynamic RAM static memory chip.

Wall Street plays a vital role in the world economy. Think of it as grease. Slimy but necessary. Yes, let's add another type of Server. Let's call finance folks **Slimers**.

Capital is needed for buildings and equipment and directors of marketing and a sales force. Even big companies need lots of capital to fund accounts payable and accounts receivable and working capital for ordering and shipping parts from China. But whose money? At what interest rate should it be lent? Or maybe a company will sell shares to raise money. But at what price?

That's what the bond market and the stock market is for—for discovering the right prices and the right interest rates based on the number of buyers and sellers. But also to get stocks or pieces of credit into the hands of those with the appropriate risk profile.

But it's not your local farmer's market—you can't just walk up to a stock market and do business. Try that at the New York Stock Exchange and large surly bouncers will throw you back out onto Wall or Broad Street. And the stock market isn't even inside the New York Stock Exchange or anywhere else. It never really was.

Instead, the stock market is just a concept. Connected people taking in a fire hose of information every nanosecond of every day and make buying and selling decisions based on the price of securities. It's controlled chaos.

I look at the stock market as a giant, pulsing, million-degrees-Fahrenheit piece of plasma—way too big for any one person to manipulate, let alone touch directly. If you get too close, you get burned.

Surrounding that giant piece of plasma is Wall Street, forming a protective ring so transactions from you and me can take place.

For a modest fee (okay, not always all that modest) Wall Street will help you find buyers of your stock, or go find someone who wants to sell theirs. Or they can round up a billion dollars for a new ethylene plant in Lubbock, Texas. Whatever it takes.

Yeah, sure, there are greedy types on Wall Street, I've worked with my fair share. And yes, the compensation scheme is lucrative. And yeah, Wall Street almost sank the world economy with their stupidity of packaging and then owning subprime mortgages.

But we need Wall Street. Innovation doesn't exist in a vacuum. It needs capital to work. Entrepreneurs are just dreamers without capital to make their dreams hit the hard pavement and zoom down the road of progress and prosperity. You can classify Wall Street as Servers or Sloppers or even Thieves if you like. The stock market is regulated and plenty of firms, especially the New York Stock Exchange, take advantage of that with outsized profits.

I kind of think of Slimers as lubrication on the gears of the economy, which would overheat and turn brittle without capital. Slimers. Come up with whatever metaphor you like, Wall Street is needed and at least some of the profits they make are of the Free Radical variety.

So what about the whole *Soylent Green* people-eating thing? Billions of dollars have been spent automating the supply chain at manufacturers. Now the opportunity is to automate the "service chain." Now that we've classified everyone, which of these jobs should you get rid of? Or at least devalue?

I'd suggest they are all up for grabs. But let's certainly start with the Thieves. They have some of the highest markups over their real economic value. That ought to be easy. Then the Sponges and the

Sloppers should be pretty easy to go after—just as Slimers, from brokers to traders, have been made obsolete by technology.

Even the normal ordinary everyday Server jobs are suspect. The person who takes your order at Starbucks (a Server who has morphed into a Slopper by calling herself a barista and raising the price)? Of course. Turn the cash register around and let me punch in my order. Groceries have already saved a bundle by creating self-checkout lines where customers scan and bag their own stuff. And for the 57 percent of customers who only ever order a "mocha latte, extra hot, no whip," just swiping a loyalty card ought to trigger that order. It's not that hard to get rid of a few jobs.

Or use voice recognition to replace their overcaffeinated morning greeting. Voice recognition not ready? Then get to work on it. Perhaps it will be the next abundance. A Free Radical recognizes opportunity.

And the poor schnook stocking the shelves at Walmart? Robotics.

Okay, the car mechanic? He's already halfway out the door with electronic sensors that tell him what's wrong and how to fix it. A connector called OBD-II that connects to onboard diagnostics already obsoletes lots of mechanics.

Plumbers? Builders? Yup and yup. C'mon, think about it. Sensors and prefab are the future. Just put your mind to it and you can figure out a way to make all these jobs toast.

And authors? Bring it on!

OKAY, LET'S GO back to basics. Remember, wealth comes from productivity. In a world where all we do is wash each other's cars, no wealth would be created. Fair enough. The economic measure of productivity is output per worker hour. Economists use fancy terms like "capital stock," which are just tools to augment workers to increase their output. Fishing net. An ox and plow. Or an assembly line. And, I don't know, even robots, I guess. More output from fewer hours produces wealth. Companies spent millions on factory gurus, Six-Sigma–smoking consultants from the 1950s all the way through the 1970s to help them squeeze gains out of workers. That's what drove the stock market and wealth creation for several decades.

That's all fine in an Industrial Age when you can actually measure worker output in the form of widgets per day, cars off the line per hour, and the like. But in a service economy filled with knowledge workers flitting around trying to produce more, uh, banking or more insurance or more satisfaction at McDonald's, the productivity game isn't so easy.

It's hard to find ways to make workers more productive. Give 'em a BlackBerry or something. Is that the way to create wealth?

I doubt it. The trick is to look under the covers to find the new type of technology-bred capital stock—and figure out what all this technology is replacing. It's not so obvious.

Microsoft Word replaced secretaries. Pretty easy, though now we have executive assistants. But a lot fewer, thanks to voice mail and calendar software and other tools. Those 800 numbers were invented because AT&T couldn't hire enough operators to handle all the collect calls to businesses.

Oracle database software replaced a lot of in-house accountants. Again, pretty easy. But what about Google? To look up all the things we currently query for would require millions of extra librarians. But we didn't hire them. We, in effect, replaced librarians that we didn't know we even needed (Say's law again?). Black-

Berrys replaced mail carriers. Sure, we still have them for junk mail and the occasional magazine, but personal communication is far faster and more productive without humans carrying letters.

ATMs replaced tellers. Computer servers replaced stock traders. Travelocity and Expedia replaced travel agents. Online trading killed stockbrokers. I can go on and on.

My point is this: get rid of humans and you have probably found a rich vein of productivity and therefore wealth. I know, I know, it sounds so awful. So Scrooge-like—fire Tiny Tim's father on Christmas Eve to generate wealth. Okay, it's not that bad. That's the goal of every economy—to increase the standard of living of its participants. If that means over a generation replacing low-skill jobs with higher-skilled careers developing more productive tools, then you are creating wealth for the entire economy.

We went from Stone Age to Iron Age to Industrial Age to Space Age and we're now firmly in the Idea Age. Wealth and success are no longer guaranteed by working long hours climbing the corporate ladder of success at Amalgamated Widgets, hand over hand with knives in the backs of your coworkers. Ideas rule. That whole Knowledge Economy thing may sound like a dripping cliché, but you'd better figure it out because it's how wealth is created today, not by assembling cars or digging for oil or financing real estate or teaching history. In fact, those who do study history are doomed to repeat it.

But what does that even mean, "Ideas Rule"?

We've done it before. Transitioning from an agricultural to an industrial economy meant automating farming—tractors, combines, better seeds, praying for rain—and it worked. Down from maybe 80 percent of American colonists working on farms, today just 3 percent of the U.S. population feeds the rest of us—so you and I don't have to get up at 5:30 in the morning to milk the chickens. That's progress with a capital P. We got rid of factory jobs, either through automation or by exporting them to China and India. Again, capital P progress, because it's really hot in those steel mills, from what I've been told. I think I saw one in a Tom Cruise movie once. We're now an economy of service workers at far greater risk of getting paper cuts than losing a limb at the mill.

But now we're in the middle of another transition, from that postindustrial "would you like those fries Supersized" world of the eighties and nineties to a more pure knowledge-based, brain-fueled something.

So what is that something?

Think about it: it's only been over the last ten years that we've gotten rid of operators and tellers and travel agents and stockbrokers and replaced them with a flat-panel screen and a mouse connected to the Internet.

Digital cameras killed Kodak film developers just like video killed the radio star.

But that's just a start. There are so many more useless jobs to get rid of! What about disc jockeys? Almost gone. But then what about tax preparers? Bookstore clerks? Cops? House painters? Magazine layout designers? Auctioneers? Dwindling guilds. Humble and lovable shoeshine boy?

In other words—humans are costly.

Again, this is progress, sure, but why stop there? Every job you can imagine is suspect—from marketing manager to chip designer to copy editor to "assistant to the regional manager" and on and on until we reach lawyers and doctors and strangle them as well. They are all toast in one way or another, replaced by smart systems that can interact with the human race faster, cheaper, and better.

It's weird, isn't it? We've been overtaught to love our fellow man, be kind to our neighbors, "c'mon people now, smile on your brother, everybody get together and try to love one another right now." But we climb the steep hill of economic growth by standing on the bloody heads that have rolled from those at obsolete jobs. (Hey, wasn't that one of the scenes in the second *Lord of the Rings*? No matter.) Gruesome, the metaphor anyway, but real. It just happens slowly enough that it's more like Chinese water torture than a flood.

But how to prepare for all this change? College, when it's not learning you how to learn, prepares students for the very jobs that Free Radicals are busy getting rid of! A Free Radical had best prepare for a world of networks and mobility and attention mining and social graphs or whatever nom du jour the social commentators come up with, and the best way is to find a set of Servers, and then eat them by rendering them obsolete.

Markets Make Better Decisions Than Managers

You WOULD THINK THAT, AFTER THE CREDIT CRISIS OF 2008, no one would trust markets ever again. But you should. Free Radicals embrace markets and learn to trust them more than their own instincts. I'm not kidding.

A few years back, needing relief from medieval churches and cutesy cafés on a trip to Prague with my wife (okay, and I was trying to figure out how to write off the airfare and all those Pilsner Urquells from the night before), I paid a call on the Prague Stock Exchange. Bet you didn't even know they had one. It was tucked in a blocky, Soviet-architecture building off the main drag. Concrete poured into a square mold with small windows blasted out. Bland as a Kansas City warehouse, it was easy to miss. No giant flag wrapped around the building or traders in funny-colored jackets milling around like at the New York Stock Exchange.

I climbed a few flights of poorly lit stairs and entered a dour, dusty, musty office. I didn't expect Dick Grasso or John Thain clapping with happy CEOs at an opening bell ceremony, but heck, this place might as well have been the Division of Motor Vehicles. I started pining for churches and stained glass windows again. The receptionist put down her Marlboro Light and took me into the stark office of the chairman of the exchange. My eyes began to tear and I had to squint to make out the chairman behind a wall of secondhand smoke. His office had one potted plant and a chair that might have seen duty in prison electrocutions. I sat down.

"Thanks for taking the time to see me," I said.

"We don't get many visitors."

The chairman had a full head of dark hair, a wrinkled face, and an ill-fitting suit; no doubt he was a district member of the Party a decade earlier. I looked for a bottle of Stoli with no luck. He gave me a quizzical, confused look. Believe me, I'm used to that look.

"I'm visiting as many exchanges around the world as I can," I lied, tempted to add the line from *Meatballs*, "armed with only a thermos of coffee and two thousand dollars cash."

"You are from Wall Street?"

"No, I live in California."

"Hollywood?"

"Close. Anyway, I was hoping to get a tour."

He started laughing. "You have already seen most of it. You met Zuzana?"

The receptionist, I assumed. "Yes?"

"Well, there you have it."

"The exchange is . . ." I started to ask.

He reached behind his desk and pulled back a curtain. Behind a sheet of Plexiglas were probably a dozen PCs, lined up in a neat row.

Of course, duh, there is no Prague Stock Exchange, not physically anyway. Just a bunch of computer servers sitting here matching trades all day. Okay, I get that. But how am I going to fill the next fifty-five minutes? My mind races.

Even after working so many years on Wall Street, I'm still numbed by its complexity—the Dow Jones Industrial Average rising and falling in seemingly random correlations to sunspots or something. Million-dollar bonuses to traders younger than that Rolling Stones T-shirt in the back of your closet. Derivatives. Rate hikes. Credit swaps. Subprime loans. Discounted free cash flow. Man, this stuff is harder than Chinese arithmetic.

I guess what intrigues me is that the Czech Republic even has stocks to trade in the first place. One day the government owns every business, bloated with beer-breath bureaucrats, and then boom! The Berlin Wall falls, Prague is wrapped in Velvet, and the next day it's capitalism? That's got to be a tricky transition. So I asked.

In Soviet-style communism, the chairman explained, the state owned everything. All of a sudden, democracy and capitalism rolled into town, and no one quite knew how to go from a system of shared public ownership to private property and a functioning economy with price discovery and resource allocation and wealth creation.

To pull this off, in the Czech Republic and lots of other former members of the Soviet Union, authorities handed out chits—an equal number to each and every citizen—which could be traded in to buy shares of companies in a series of auctions—the state-owned banks, oil refineries, phone companies, electric utilities, auto manufacturers, and so on.

As a Czech citizen, you could participate in the auctions, or you could just sell the chits to someone else, which lots of people did around Christmastime. An unofficial "street market" for chits came and went. It took a number of auctions to get the correct price for each of the state businesses to move into private hands.

Pay no attention to those PCs behind the curtain, Dorothy, but they were loaded with code to match buyers and sellers. At the New York Stock Exchange, we (still) have some human traders screaming out buy and sell orders to get to the right price for IBM shares. Here in Eastern Europe, they eliminated the middlemen entirely, letting software do the price discovery and matching. Once the right price was reached, all the chits turned into shares of stock in the Czech Republic's industries. Then, a high-speed data line was set up connecting to the Frankfurt Stock Exchange and foreign money slowly started to show up for shares of Czech companies, infusing outside money into the system. It took a few years, but eventually, as trading increased on their electronic-only exchange, the value of each company was set by its prospects for growth and profits and the market eventually transferred ownership completely from the state to individuals.

My host paused and smiled and continued, "And then, with magic, companies start to make money, profits. They cut—how you say—fat?" as he grabbed his belly, "and stocks go up and they get more money to grow."

MARKETS GET A bad name—stock markets anyway. Mostly because they are so volatile and do unexplained things—like going up when bad news comes out, putting a huge value on Pets.com, and crashing precipitously every once in a while.

No doubt, the stock market trades to inflict the maximum

amount of pain. If everyone thinks it's going to go up, it's sure to drop. Why is that? Well, the market measures sentiment every day, and figures out what everyone thinks, a consensus if you will, and for the most part prices that into the market. But then some of its inputs change—profits are worse or inflation has been tamed—and the market moves, well before the consensus has figured out what has changed. It's nerve-wracking, everyone second-guessing themselves as they get whacked by the market again and again.

But the stock market performs the most important function in a capitalist system—it mercilessly allocates capital to those that deserve it and starves those that don't. That's pretty much it. IPOs and options and collateralized debt obligation derivatives are all, well, derivatives of this allocation task.

It's almost always government policy that misallocates capital and causes markets to go haywire. Be forewarned, there is no such thing as a perfect market, but you can get pretty close.

Free Radicals should embrace markets. Not just stock markets, but all market mechanisms, because the markets will do the work for you, pointing the path toward the best places to allocate capital. Markets make better decisions than people.

So how do markets work? Let's start with the stock market—which is nothing but a market that trades profits.

Let me go back to the fish from the Productivity Rule. That fishing net company can only grow so large without buying machines to automate the manufacture of your new design—I'll call it the Net Net. You're making good profits, but you'd have to wait five years to earn enough to be able to afford one machine. Instead, you sell off some of your future profits to raise capital by selling shares in your company. Seems like a fair trade.

But how much of your company do you sell to raise, say, $5

million? How much stock, if I arbitrarily divide my profits into 1 million "shares"? If I can show that with $5 million I can make $2 million in profits next year and then $3.5 million and then $5 million, maybe, just maybe, I can convince someone that the company is worth $20 million or ten times next year's profits. And how, pray tell, do I sucker someone into giving me $5 million of their hard-earned money in exchange for a piece of paper saying they own a quarter of my profits?

Pretty simple. Stocks are worth the sum of all future profits discounted back to today. Money today is worth more than the same amount of money tomorrow, because of inflation and whatever other risks you want to pile on. So I sum $2 million, plus (assuming a 20 percent discount rate) 80 percent of the $3.5 million and then 65 percent of the $5 million and so on. Yes, this requires math, but if you go out enough years and discount it back, the multiplier gets pretty small and you are no longer adding much in, so it only takes the first several years of profits to get a close approximation.

Anyway, lo and behold, my company, if my projections of $2 per share ($2 million divided by 1 million shares) in profits are right, really is worth $20 million. So I sell 250,000 shares at $20 a share (ten times next year's profits) for the $5 million and keep the other 750,000 for myself. And on day one, the stock trades on the open market at $20.

Open market? Sure. From the old European bourses to the New York Stock Exchange to entirely electronic markets, people with capital buy and sell these shares because they think they are undervalued or overvalued. Maybe expectations for future profits change. Maybe the rate at which future earnings are discounted back goes up because of fears of inflation. Or maybe a war starts and no one is buying nets or a hurricane hits and kills all the fish.

The price of the shares is going to go up and down based on changing expectations. It's a rare day that shares of a stock don't change
in price. Not by edict, but by more buyers than sellers driving the
price up or more sellers than buyers driving it down.

The stock market does this calculation every minute of every
day it's open. If it thinks the market for the Net Net is bigger than
originally thought, expectations for profits go up, maybe to $3 per
share instead of $2, and all of a sudden others start buying shares in
the open market, driving the price up to $30 to own a share of these
soon-to-be-larger profits. Trading in the open market is all about
profit expectations, not absolutes. On the other hand, if someone
is caught making fake puka shells, which is the local currency,
then inflation expectations rise and the discount rate goes up and
now investors are only willing to pay seven times my $2 per share
profit projection. My stock falls to $14 per share. Ouch. (By the way,
you've just passed a college-level corporate finance course!)

Markets are all about price discovery. Those shares are traded
back and forth, bumping up and down until they settle at the right
price, whatever that right price really means. More subjective than
objective.

And who are these "people with capital"? You, me, banks, mutual funds, foreign governments—the more the merrier. All that
matters is that lots of people express their opinion on how they
think my company is going to do, profit-wise, by trading shares
based on that opinion. Like magic, the stock will seek the right
price and the market will efficiently allocate capital.

At $30, I can raise another $5 million for another machine
and only sell off one sixth of the company instead of a quarter.
Or maybe someone else introduces the Triple Net and my stock
drops to $10, a signal that the market is starving me of capital be-

cause it thinks my sales are going to drop and my expenses are too high. Of course, with the stock down, and me starved of capital, I'll quickly trim costs and lay off workers and scramble to design the even more productive Quad Net and I'll be off to the races again.

Free Radicals take note. No one person makes the decision if I get capital or not. The market decides, en masse. No politician can pick winners or losers (though they can regulate the fishing net market and distort stock prices).

But be warned, ye old Free Radicals . . . the market is a heartless bitch. That's its most important attribute. It couldn't care less about people and job security and benefits and feelings and whether a town is going to be ravaged from job losses. It neatly and efficiently and heartlessly allocates capital.

And thank goodness it does. Because no one else has the fortitude to step up and tell a company that they've got to lay off 30 percent of their workers right now! Free markets do this well.

Of course, there may not be any such thing as a free market. Brokers need licenses, making them Sponges. Information doesn't quite disseminate as smoothly as it should. The brother-in-law of the head of sales at some widget company will know well before you do that business is better than anyone thinks. Price discovery is not always done well. But eventually, it does get done, and capital either rushes in or runs away.

Great investors are taught to listen to the market. Each tick of the tape has something to say about expectations for growth, inflation, policy changes, and looming recessions. As I mentioned before, the stock market is like a giant mass of pulsing plasma. It's way too big for any one person to manipulate, let alone touch directly. Instead, millions of us provide input with our buying and selling decisions. When it's at its most efficient, with buyers and sellers neatly matched up at the right price, it's a pretty good predictor. When it's not, chaos is sure to follow. In effect, the stock market is doing price discovery as well as a game of hot potato, getting stocks into the correct hands with the right risk profile.

Eugene Fama, a University of Chicago business school professor, proposed an efficient-market hypothesis back in 1969. Fama suggested that a market in which prices always "fully reflect" available information is called "efficient."

Fama believed that a market that is liquid enough (lots of buyers and sellers meeting in the market and sharing price information) and that can be arbitraged easily (someone can quickly take advantage of price differentials by buying or selling) will be efficient enough so that any information and investor expectations will be quickly reflected in securities prices. Oh yeah, and no trader will be able to put together an automated strategy to achieve riskless profits.

Forty years later, the debate rages over whether markets are efficient or not. But of course they're not, just like a physics experiment where you assume a frictionless surface that doesn't exist in real life. You have to assume that markets are mostly efficient. But they're never fully efficient—there is always something adding friction. People think there are riskless profits, until whatever is stuck comes unstuck and then watch out below.

The stock market peaked on October 9, 2007, with the Dow at 14,164. Then the credit crisis and a Lehman Brothers bankruptcy sent the market into a free fall, bottoming out at 6,547 only seventeen months later. Contrast this with a decade earlier, when the dot-com-laden NASDAQ peaked at 5,048, only to bottom coincidentally on October 9, 2002, at 1,114. Back then, companies like Pets.com were going to fundamentally reshape the economy in the new millennium into a Kool-Aid-induced nirvana of spectacular growth and well-being. Or something like that.

No one would blame you for thinking the market is a textbook delusional paranoid schizophrenic, not knowing the difference between the real and the unreal. And you'd be right. But you'd miss a valuable lesson. Misallocation of capital is everywhere and anywhere a victim of bad policy.

The late-nineties Internet lovefest was crazy enough, driven by misguided telecom reform in 1996. Bad policy meant capital got overallocated, and then some, as a combination of IPO lockups (insiders have to wait 180 days before they can sell), NASDAQ trading restraints involving "momos" (mutual funds that only buy on momentum, i.e., only stocks that are going up), and day traders turned greedy drove up stock prices of every company with dotcom in its name for no fundamental reasons. Wall Street trading was broken. And then insult to injury saw Alan Greenspan and the Federal Reserve flood the system with money over fears the banks' computers would freeze up when the world went from 1999 to 2000 and we would see a bank run as people closed accounts and withdrew to all cash. It never happened. All that Fed money ended up in the stock market. Mopping up that money burst the bubble.

Yes, the market tanked hard. Unfortunately, the post–9/11 world of accounting scandals brought us costly legislation in Sarbanes-Oxley, which decoupled research from investment banking, and the Federal Reserve with its nightmare fears of deflation ushered in a long era of cheap credit. Fannie and Freddie fanned the flames and then fizzled and failed. Instead of finishing what the dot-com era started to deliver, a productive, wealth-producing economy, capital—especially from university endowments—was seduced into the financial lair of private equity and real estate mortgages.

Trillions were pumped into unneeded housing stock. And leveraged buyouts reigned as, as late as 2007, one Blackstone private equity fund raised some $26 billion, almost as much money as all of venture capital firms did that year. With few exceptions, no real wealth was created in almost a decade, from 2000 to 2010.

This financial seduction, of course, didn't end well, with the market halving, bottoming on March 9, 2009, with fears of a wholesale financial system meltdown. Blame whoever you want: greedy bankers or those who took out liar loans, but the root was bad policy.

Sure, emotions play a big role. Momentum investors convince themselves that stocks that go up will keep going up, probably because subconsciously they know the market is inefficient, that is, someone or his brother-in-law must know something. But in effect, it's the momos that make the market inefficient, thinking they have a riskless trade when in reality it's some piece of bad policy that becomes obvious in retrospect. Legions of economists study things like "animal spirits" (the idea that human psychology drives markets) but need to look no further than stupidity wrapped in a momentum investing strategy.

So there is short-term inefficient and long-term efficient. You can argue until you're blue in the face, but all I can say is thank goodness markets aren't efficient. Why? Because it allows those of us who can analyze these markets to figure out future information about the direction of industries and companies and profits (with the help of, say, these 12 Rules) well before it is available, before it is actual information rather than a really good guess, a gut feel, a hallucination maybe. But we can get there first before anyone else knows anything and wipe up as future profit information is "fully reflected."

Strip away all the supposed genius of Wall Street—"Well, Maria, there were more buyers than sellers today"—and you get Prague—so simple it can be boiled down to its core element. Companies make profits. Markets value those profits and set the price for the enterprise so they can raise more money to grow. The stock market allocates precious capital to companies it thinks can maximize profits and starves those that can't.

In other words, the stock market is democracy's half-evil henchman, whose tool is the size of the carrot, not the use of the stick. The tenets of capitalism's great economists, from Adam Smith's Invisible Hand to Joseph Schumpeter's Creative Destruction and Gordon Gekko's Greed Is Good, are all powerful concepts, but it's profits and the stock market that carry out the dirty work. No Five-Year Plans. All men are created equal, but a few of you need to be canned and retrained so progress can happen again. New industries get funded and start hiring again. But which ones? The ones with the best prospects for profits.

Remember, markets don't create wealth. They allow for price discovery and for productivity to be priced into the value of companies.

BUT ENOUGH ABOUT the stock market for now. This Rule is not about beating the stock market (although I say go for it); it's about Free Radicals using markets for themselves. To allocate things—in your business, in a service, in your life, whatever.

Because markets make decisions better than managers.

It's about price discovery—inputs from lots and lots of people to get to the right price. Managers have biases or they haven't had their coffee yet or are hungover or who knows what personal problems afflict them. Don't trust managers; trust markets to get to the correct price.

Markets are about trading stuff; it doesn't have to be just stocks (which is just trading in the profits of companies). Free Radicals can trade goods, services, and especially information—anything of value—and let the market set the value. It could be open outcry markets, electronic trading, auctions, reverse auctions, modified Dutch auctions, who cares. Just make sure there are participants.

The stock market is the largest in size and volume, but it's all relative. Stock markets are more efficient than the market for, I don't know, automobiles or wine or cherry Slurpees. What I'm suggesting is to create a market price for everything you do—for your products and services, for your employee ratings and raises, for customer service, everything. Have enough information, some definition of profit, so that everything can trade. Your little mini-markets will allocate resources better than any other method.

It could be internal prices or external prices with your customers.

The price will be set by more than one person, the masses out at the edge, and therefore will be more reflective of actual profits—however profits are actually defined—than one person sitting in a room making up the "price." It could be a transfer price between divisions, the price to use a conference room during peak hours, whatever.

eBay made an entire business out of price discovery and then closing the financial part of the transaction. Not always an efficient market, but it was better than going to garage sales and estate markets trying to figure out the right price. Sadly, eBay didn't create a market for their own fees—raising them instead of lowering them—and stopped growing.

StubHub, which eBay eventually bought, does the same thing for sports and concert tickets. I mastered the art as a kid with no money, showing up right before a concert started and buying "distressed" tickets from someone whose friend didn't show up so they were about to eat them. You see the adult version of this outside of every major league baseball game. Scalpers know the right price much better than the average fan scrambling to get inside. The electronic version is much more, though not perfectly, liquid. I waste hours (which has its own price) on these services hunting for mispriced tickets. They are getting harder to find.

Google built a whole business on market pricing. It began with a fast and comprehensive search engine but no real business model. Employee number nine, Salar Kamangar, all of twenty-two years old, was tasked with Google's early revenue generation, along with Eric Veach. The two decided to put links down the side of the search results page, along with "see your ad here." The first company to buy a link ad sold lobsters. Not knowing what to charge, Kamangar and Veach wrote code, AdWords, that priced the ads via auction. In other words, customers set the price.

In April of 2003, Google bought Applied Semantics and their automated content-targeted ad technology called AdSense, to up the ante, but the basic market for ads still works today. The price is never wrong if customers set the price by competing with each other. If there are a dozen companies selling big-screen LCD TVs, the one that gives up what I calculate is half of their gross profits to Google gets the top spot and probably the sale. An ad salesperson might have been happy to get $10, when the right price was $75. At $20-plus billion in revenue, Google extracts top dollar by using markets to do the price discovery for them.

By the way, this doesn't mean there are no people involved;

Google has a 4,000-person ad sales force, but that is as much lead generation and customer service, and their self-service ad market sets all the prices.

Markets work for information too. According to their Web site, Digg "is a place for people to discover and share content from anywhere on the web. From the biggest online destinations to the most obscure blog, Digg surfaces the best stuff as voted on by our users. You won't find editors at Digg—we're here to provide a place where people can collectively determine the value of content . . ."

Digg got in some trouble a while back for rigging some of the voting, selecting a few Super Users who could censor items. Again, no market is perfectly efficient; Digg must have had problems with spam or hate speech and had to act to clean it up. But whatever inefficiency you introduce is going to come back to bite you in the end. Other sites, like Reddit, deploy market voting in other ways.

Politicians have figured out the power of markets as well. The various proposals for cap and trade to create a market for carbon dioxide emissions are a perfect example. With cap and trade, someone sets the amount of emissions each firm is allowed and then trading begins between those that need more emission permits and those that have extras because they reduced emissions. But this is flawed in that people, not the market, set the actual cap or maximum amount of emissions, creating an almost artificial market for extra carbon credits to trade until the right price is set. The more human intervention overriding the market, the tougher true price discovery becomes.

Lots of companies are playing around with prediction markets, using the Intelligence at the Edge and running surveys and varying pricing to figure out what people will pay for new products.

Like it or not, markets will be inserted into more and more of our lives and Free Radicals ought to be the ones doing it, driving markets, making them happen everywhere. I can't tell you all the things that will be market driven. Think it through. Transactions, decisions, everything that has to allocate your money and your time and your energy and your attention can have a market applied to it. It won't be long until you ask your friends to vote on Facebook not only on what you should do this afternoon, but who you date or when you have your next child. I'm not sure that's the best use of markets, but if there is a price for something, there will be a market to discover that price.

Embrace Exceptionalism

THE BABY BOOMER GENERATION IS GENERALLY DEFINED AS all those people born between 1943 and 1960 who are (often correctly) stereotyped as self-indulgent and workaholics. Generation X, generally defined as those born between 1961 and 1981, are characterized as unmotivated slackers and hopeless cynics. These are followed by Generation Y, born from 1982 to the early 1990s, who are optimistic, socially responsible multitaskers.

I hate stereotypes like this, but I'm going to pile on. There is no Generation Z, but instead there is the Trophy Generation—those born from 1990 to present. They were raised with the community mantra: No matter what, everyone gets a trophy. We are all the same. And all of us are winners and entitled to the spoils that automatically accrue to winners.

Yeah, right. Free Radicals should quickly shed this thinking.

From the French Revolution came the expression *liberté, égalité, fraternité*—freedom, equality, and brotherhood. Pretty catchy, actually. You might recall that I saw it on a plate at that rich French guy's house. Too bad those three simple words have spun minds in bizarre directions over the two centuries since they were first uttered, and have killed wealth a few too many times. With the Trophy Generation, they're back.

Let's leave aside *fraternité*/brotherhood for now. It's a tad touchy-feely, but to me brotherhood means that we are all in this together. A "do unto others" kind of message that needed to be said after chopping off the heads of French royalty.

And no one can be against liberty and freedom. Free markets, free people, freedom to be an individual (oops, except when we are a *fraternité*), freedom fries. Freedom's just another word for . . . being unbound, to pursue what we want, to reach for the stars, to improve our lot and on and on. To be a Free Radical.

But with *égalité*/equality, I wonder if the world has misunderstood or misrepresented the whole thing. How can we be free if we are all forced to be equal? Doesn't that imply that we are all only as good as the worst of us? Perhaps I've got to believe the French meant equal opportunity. At least, I hope they did; if they didn't, they deserve the European-style socialism they've fallen into.

Equal opportunity means no one is held back or has their freedom restricted, because of who they are, their upbringing, their sex, race, sexual orientation, disability, if they are any good at sports (I hear one investment banking firm never hires fat people who can't ski), and whatever else.

You see, we are not equal. Forget this way of thinking. It tries to squash Free Radicals. Forget the politically correct tropes about the dangers of IQ tests and aptitude measuring. Some are smarter than others. If you went to high school, you know this. If you work at a company, you know this. So quit trying to say we are all equal. I've had female bosses who were a heck of a lot smarter than I am. So there, that proves it!

Equal opportunity, yes. Equal, well, no.

And forget all the mumbo jumbo you read in the popular press that we really are all equal but some of us have advantages.

New Yorker magazine columnist and über-author Malcolm Gladwell has written tomes proving that someone's success is just an accident or a freak. In *Blink*, he convinces us that we are prejudiced. In *Outliers*, Gladwell tries to persuade us that success has more to do with being in the right place at the right time, and putting in ten thousand hours of practice, than with having any inherent ability. In *Guns, Germs, and Steel*, Jared Diamond spends 425 pages (with really small letters on them) arguing that the real reason the Europeans beat out the South Americans and the Africans was because their continent was wide, east to west, with similar climates, instead of tall and narrow, north to south, with varying climates. And then something about llamas (there, now you don't have to read it!).

The smart Hispanic kid from East L.A. should have the same opportunity as the lockjaw preppie from Connecticut to get into Harvard, start a company, go public, and be a CEO. Even more so if the Hispanic is smarter than the preppie. The trick is equal opportunity, not some one-size-fits-all *égalité*.

All that progress over the last one hundred years has not come exclusively from the children or grandchildren of the successful types from the previous generation. Quite the opposite. According to the University of Michigan's Panel Study of Income Dynamics, 67 percent of white children born between 1967 and 1971 have incomes higher than their parents after adjusting for inflation, meaning real wealth creation. And 63 percent of black children from that same time period have higher incomes than their parents.

The next wave of exceptional folks, the next set of inventors and productivity Creators, the next Free Radicals, may also come from humble beginnings, like Edison and Einstein. Or maybe they'll come from Park Avenue or Berkeley Square or Bel Air. It doesn't matter where they come from; we have to embrace them. Canadian economist Reuven Brenner referred to them as "the Vital Few." I think he nailed it.

So simple—Embrace Exceptionalism.

The exceptional, the Vital Few, the Makes versus the Takes, are the ones destroying the past and creating our future—increasing our wealth and paving the road for the next exceptional crew.

WONDERING IF THERE was something a bit more scientific than my own gut feelings about this whole exceptionalism thing, I hunted around for someone who has worked with tons of really smart and even off-the-charts exceptional people. I found what I was looking for with Bill Raduchel, who has lived in the technology world since before there really was one.

As a Harvard PhD and professor, Raduchel taught some of the brightest kids in the world. And he was smart enough to leave academia for the real world—he was the CFO and CIO at Sun Microsystems during their barn-burning growth years in the 1990s. In 1999, Raduchel joined America Online as their CTO until the Time Warner merger. He has since worked with dozens of mostly tech firms, from start-ups to public companies. In other words, Raduchel has been around smart people his whole life.

I got into a conversation with him at a conference we both

attended and he kept talking about these smart people, the half of one percent who really matter. From what I heard, it sounded a lot like what I knew about the Vital Few, so I met up with him afterward and pressed him for what he really meant.

"When we met before, you mentioned something about the half of one percent—the smartest—as being the most important to wealth and living standards and that kind of stuff. I've thought about that a lot, and I intuitively agree, but what do you really mean by that?"

"There is a fascinating book by the late Maurice Halstead which covers a lot of this."

He was referring to *Elements of Software Science*, published in May of 1977.

"My perspective on intelligence," Raduchel continued, "is that there are four main parameters . . ."

"Meaning four measures, like IQ?" I asked.

"No, no, more characteristics of human intelligence, less top-down measures, but more to understand the differences in each of us."

"Okay."

"First, there is the Stroud number. Think of it as something like the CPU clock speed. How fast our brains work. Most studies I read found a relatively narrow range of ability, say three to one. This is significant, but I have met some brilliant but seemingly slow thinkers."

John M. Stroud was a psychologist who focused on the processing rate of the brain, laid out in his 1967 paper "The Fine Structure of Psychological Time." To Stroud, a "moment" was the time it took the human brain to perform some task, some "elementary discrimination." A Stroud number is the number of these moments per second, which he guesstimated (in 1966, I suspect brain scans were not what they are today!) at between five and twenty, or a four-to-one range. Close enough to three-to-one.

"And I know a lot of quick-thinking dopes," I say, trying to agree with him.

Ignoring me, Bill went on: "Second, human memory appears to be organized in something that resembles linked lists or chunks or containers of information. When you have a chunk open, you appear to know everything that is in it. Humans appear to average seven chunks open at any one time, which is why U.S. telephone numbers have seven digits. However, this number too varies but in a narrow range—something like three to twelve is what I remember."

All I could think of is being told as a kid that I couldn't chew gum and ride a bike at the same time.

"Meaning we usually can daydream or noodle over seven things at the same time?" I asked. Uh-oh. My mind starts to wander and now I'm wondering why I have 12 Rules and a Bonus Rule instead of just seven.

"That's right, but some of us can handle almost twice as much, which makes a difference when you are doing some complex task: writing software, manipulating genes, things like that."

And hopefully when reading books.

"Third," Bill went on, "original thought appears to be Darwinian in the following sense—the brain is really good at evaluating, so when you have to generate a thought, you grab a template— which is why anchors matter—and then make random changes in it before sending it to an evaluator which decides yes or no."

"You mean a template of some existing thought?" I asked.

"Right. This is why you hear yourself saying things for the first time when you speak it. Using brain scans, you can count how many thought generators a person has, and again you find a narrow range like two to ten, with an average around five. None of this data is from that large a sample of the population, of course."

"So we have clock speed and number of chunks and number of thought generators, and that's enough to explain the difference in intelligence?"

"Almost. What really varies a lot is the size of a memory chunk. This is what Halstead modestly called the 'Halstead length.' He created some arbitrary metrics but found that the average was two hundred and fifty—which is about fifty lines of software code—Fortran back then. However, people varied dramatically here, and the very best programmers had lengths of sixty thousand plus."

"Sixty thousand versus the average of two hundred and fifty?"

"That's right. So here is an attribute which varies by a factor of maybe one hundred across people, instead of just three-to-one or four-to-one. The longer the Halstead length, the greater the problem you can comprehend, the richer the data structure you can employ."

"So it's not just how fast or how many strings of thoughts you can move around, it's how deep your thoughts are . . ."

"I once had a fascinating airplane flight with the author Morris West comparing how novelists are so much like great programmers, and the answer is a large Halstead length. To comprehend something, anyone must reduce it to one or more chunks, each of which is less than one Halstead length long. Then you need to add summary layers until you get to one chunk. If the complexity of something is, say, fifty thousand in Halstead length, some people will need one chunk. However, an average person will need two hundred to start with and then say another fifty in summary layers. This is a dramatic difference in understanding a complex problem and effectiveness in solving it. Some are capable, based on long Halstead lengths, while most are not."

I started wondering if he also meant not just novelists, but non-fiction writers as well, but Bill kept going.

"This is why the productivity of the top fraction of one percent is so important. The top one half of one percent can do the design, and then they can empower others to work on the pieces. It's the big thought—the design—that is so important."

So there it is. The exceptional and those who work with or for or near the exceptional are the ones who drive productivity. Eat that, Gladwell.

As I drove back home, I had this slightly confused feeling. That's not new, of course; I often live on the corner of Scrambled and Confused. But this was caused by something said in passing. Anchors—"that's why anchors matter—templates that we change before sending them to an evaluator."

So I did some digging. Anchors are one of those behavioral psychology concepts to explain how we all make decisions. An anchor is a suggestion or maybe a visualization of how to start to think about something, with the idea that it can be modified to fit the situation and perhaps the anchor makes its way into behavior. Hypnotists use anchors to get you to do things. But so do your parents and your priest or rabbi and certainly your boss. It makes sense. Who has any idea how to confront situations unless there is some anchor of honesty or morality or self-interest or just kindness that influences what we do? Entire wings of psychology departments exist to study this stuff. And now so do businesses and society. Richard Thaler and Cass Sunstein wrote *Nudge*, a book about how governments can act with "libertarian paternalism" to influence people's behavior, to nudge them away from making poor decisions. Of course, who decides what is right or wrong, good or bad?

Andrew Ferguson wrote an April 2010 piece in *The Weekly Standard* aptly titled "Nudge Nudge, Wink Wink," pointing out that many of the favorite behavioral economics studies are done by grad students observing paid volunteer undergraduates doing trivial tasks, and arguing that this is hardly a basis for making large-scale policy recommendations for a better society.

This is true of much of what is said in the "pop economics" business. Cite a study to prove some bizarre point, and then ignore all other studies or counterexamples that would easily disprove the point while looking down at anyone who argues with you, standing behind "the literature."

No one wants you to be exceptional, or to believe that anyone exceptional even exists. Ignore them all. While you invent the future, they will continue to carve up the alleged fixed-size pie among all the equals.

As it turns out, Sunstein took on the role of head of the Office of Information and Regulatory Affairs in the Obama administration, to be a nudge to all of us, as if the government can really decide what is bad versus what is good. Ah, perhaps the message is that government is exceptional, and that the rest of us are just its unwashed flock. Yikes.

By the way, when Napoleon came to power he dropped *égalité* and *fraternité* from the national motto. He replaced it with *Liberté, Ordre public*. Freedom and public order. Didn't work out so well.

So HOW DO YOU find the exceptional? Or prove to companies that you yourself are exceptional? It's getting harder and harder. Like it or not, colleges are the gateway.

In northern North Carolina, butting right up against the Virginia border, sits Rockingham County. The only college to be found in the area is the Rockingham Community College. Still, the scramble to get into the best colleges and universities, and the schools' ability to charge fifty grand or more in annual tuition, have their roots right here.

At one time, most of the electricity provided in North Carolina was generated by Duke Power. In 1948, in order to meet booming electricity demand from post World War II industrialization, Duke built two coal-burning power plants at a new site on the Dan River near the town of Draper. Costing $15 million, they were, for a time anyway, the largest boilers in the Duke Power system.

Lots of jobs were created building and running these power plants—many of them backbreaking jobs in Duke's labor department. This being the pre–Civil Rights era South, blacks were relegated to the labor department while the four other so-called operating departments—coal handling, operations, maintenance, and laboratory—were whites only. Promotions were almost always from within departments, based on seniority. The highest-paying job in the labor department paid less than the lowest-paying job in the rest of the plant.

In 1964, Title VII of the Civil Rights Act codified into law the end of discrimination based on race. Duke Power moved a little slowly. On July 2, 1965, not coincidentally the effective date of Title VII, Duke Power instituted a requirement that, to be hired into one of the higher-paying operating departments, in addition to a high school diploma, prospective employees needed to score in the upper half of two aptitude tests: the Wonderlic Personnel Test for intelligence, and the Bennett Mechanical Comprehension Test.

Of the ninety-six employees at the Dan River plants, fourteen were black, and all, as you can guess, worked in the labor department. In March 1966, thirteen of them filed a complaint with the

Equal Employment Opportunity Commission. The case, *Griggs v. Duke Power*, wound its way through the courts—district court, the Court of Appeals, and finally in December 1970, the Supreme Court of the United States. Justice may be blind but, man, is it slow.

The EEOC had found that in 1966, 58 percent of whites passed the Wonderlic and Bennett aptitude tests, while only 6 percent of blacks scored above the median.

Chief Justice Warren Burger delivered the Court's unanimous opinion in March 1971. This pretty much sums it up:

> On the record before us, neither the high school completion requirement nor the general intelligence test is shown to bear a demonstrable relationship to successful performance of the jobs for which it was used. Both were adopted, as the Court of Appeals noted, without meaningful study of their relationship to job-performance ability. Rather, a vice president of the Company testified, the requirements were instituted on the Company's judgment that they generally would improve the overall quality of the work force.
>
> The evidence, however, shows that employees who have not completed high school or taken the tests have continued to perform satisfactorily and make progress in departments for which the high school and test criteria are now used.
>
> The promotion record of present employees who would not be able to meet the new criteria thus suggests the possibility that the requirements may not be needed even for the limited purpose of preserving

the avowed policy of advancement within the Company. In the context of this case, it is unnecessary to reach the question whether testing requirements that take into account capability for the next succeeding position or related future promotion might be utilized upon a showing that such long-range requirements fulfill a genuine business need. In the present case the Company has made no such showing.

Burger goes on:

Nothing in the Act precludes the use of testing or measuring procedures; obviously they are useful. What Congress has forbidden is giving these devices and mechanisms controlling force unless they are demonstrably a reasonable measure of job performance. Congress has not commanded that the less qualified be preferred over the better qualified simply because of minority origins. Far from disparaging job qualifications as such, Congress has made such qualifications the controlling factor, so that race, religion, nationality, and sex become irrelevant. What Congress has commanded is that any tests used must measure the person for the job and not the person in the abstract.

WHAT DOES THIS have to do with college? Just about everything.

Since *Griggs v. Duke Power*, corporate America has backed away from just about any aptitude or intelligence test for prospective employees for fear of being sued under Title VII. Crazy, isn't it?

But James Taranto at *The Wall Street Journal* figured it out. James used to edit op-ed pieces I would submit to the *Journal* years ago. One had a throwaway line that Silicon Valley had higher scores on the math segment of the SAT tests than Wall Street. This turned into a long discussion with James about the value of colleges during one of many long nights in New York exploring small bars and fine cigars, where I found out, among other things, that he had higher SAT scores than me, damn, and never finished college. He wrote a terrific op-ed piece of his own in 2007 called "Disparate but Not Serious," pointing out that, unlike corporations held back by employment law and Title VII, colleges are allowed to test all they want.

SATs are, after all, the Scholastic APTITUDE Test. Duh.

Unlike companies, colleges can come up with whatever rigorous admission process they want, looking at SAT scores, high school grades, sports, afterschool activities, interviews, financial aid requirements. And they don't even have to tell you why they rejected your sorry butt and you'd be better off taking classes at Rockingham Community College.

Taranto's money quote is as follows: "The higher-education industry and corporate employers have formed a symbiotic relationship in which the former profits by acting as the latter's gatekeeper and shield against civil-rights lawsuits." Corporations have no legal way of testing just how smart you are, so they rely on colleges and universities to do their screening for them.

STILL, THERE ARE sneaky loopholes to find the true Free Radicals out there. I have more than a few friends who were forced to be interviewed by a psychiatrist before being offered a job. That sounds like cheating, but I suppose screening for multiple personalities or, say, fear of cubicles, isn't covered by Title VII.

So lots of companies that are in desperate need of really smart people but are unable to test for it directly just ask bizarre questions, hoping not so much for the right answer, but for some insight into a candidate's intelligence in the way they approach the question. Here's one I hear gets asked at Microsoft: How many golf balls can fit in a school bus? What this has to do with writing software is a bit unclear to me, but they ask anyway.

The answer, by the way, is 3 million, which is probably the right answer to most questions. A bus is about 50 feet long by 10 feet wide by 6 feet high, and so has around 3,000 cubic feet of volume. A golf ball is 1½ inches in diameter, let's call it 1.2 inches or a tenth of a foot, so its volume is one one-thousandth of a cubic foot, divided into 3,000 is 3 million golf balls. Close enough anyway, or at least close enough to explain why Microsoft software has so many bugs in it since they are asking these stupid questions rather than testing if anyone either knows or is smart enough to know how to write software.

Other questions include: How are M&M's made? How would you design a coffee machine for an automobile? How many manhole covers are in the USA?

Google goes one better. They put up billboards around the Bay Area with a bizarre puzzle that only PhDs in some obscure branch of non-Euclidian algebraic topology or some such thing know how to solve, the answer to which directs them to a Google Web page with instructions on how to apply for a job. At least that's what I heard it meant. I think it was really meant to make everyone else in the Bay Area feel stupid that they couldn't work at Google.

Still, it's something. Employers aren't charities. In our economy, companies are in business to make money, to make a return on your brain waves, paying your salary and providing other incentives (can you say stock options?) to use your brain waves instead of someone else's.

But as James Taranto suggests, colleges act as employers' gate-keepers and shields, meaning that college has become a requirement, not an option. Another great interview question for Microsoft or anyone else: Explain the Law of Unintended Consequences.

THERE ARE A lot more exceptional people than those who got 2400 on their SATs or can write code in their sleep to turn your browser into a stock trading portal. They are all over the place, and they might even be you!

But if your Halstead length is only 220, use all of your chunks to cozy up to those who are exceptional—hire them, work for them, learn from them, draft in their ever upward path. You don't have to invent Google or Genentech or Goldman Sachs, but you can appreciate how great those firms are and other soon-to-be-great firms will be.

While you are forced to go to college and while entrenched corporations and governments are nudging you, bending your mind to act as they see fit, my suggestion is to ignore all of it. Be, or at least find, exceptional people who can both see and lead the way to great things. Governments may think the idea of putting cable TV franchises out of business is bad, even though society in general may benefit greatly. Stick with the Rules, not the rulers.

Just whatever you do, as a Free Radical, embrace exceptionalism.

Be a Market Entrepreneur and Attack Political Entrepreneurs

MOST OF THE RULES SO FAR HAVE BEEN ABOUT FINDING the next big thing. The last set of rules can certainly help you find big things, but they're really about how to leverage them once you find them, how to turn big things into big wealth.

And the right type of wealth, for you and for society.

While you, a Free Radical, are out there busting your hump, making something cheaper, expanding its usage, increasing productivity, fending off fierce competition, and hoping to turn a profit along the way, there are those who, through the stroke of a pen, make a killing doing absolutely nothing of value. These "political entrepreneurs" leverage their political power to own something and then tax the crap out of the rest of us to use it. Political power instead of competition.

Sure, we can all aspire to be political entrepreneurs, but you're either born into it, or are sleazy enough to pay someone off to become one. And sure, you can get rich and then overpay public relation firms and make huge charitable contributions to clean up your story to the masses, after robbing them blind. But you will not be a Free Radical.

In 2007 and again in 2010, Carlos Slim Helú became the richest man in the world, passing Bill Gates both times. But this Mexican "businessman," if that's what you want to call him, did nothing more than buy out Telmex, the government-mandated monopoly phone company. He controls 90 percent of the phone lines in Mexico, and through ownership of Telcel, 80 percent of Mexican cell phone users send him a monthly check. He didn't invent anything. He doesn't drive down prices. There is little innovation. And why should there be? He is milking this franchise for all it's worth. Carlo Slim Helú is not a Free Radical. I'm sure Mexico is proud of its wealthy "entrepreneur," but he's no such thing, having taxed his already poor countrymen even further into poverty. Nice guy.

Easy money forever. But then again, maybe not. Because for every stroke of the pen, for every piece of legislation, for every paid-off congressman, there now exists a price umbrella that overvalues what he or any political entrepreneur is doing. Real entrepreneurs, "market entrepreneurs," recognize the price-to-value gap and jump in. Ignoring legislation, they innovate, disintermediate, compete, stay up all night coding, and offer something better and cheaper until the market starts to shift.

Author and Loyola University professor Thomas DiLorenzo defined it best: "A political entrepreneur succeeds primarily by influencing government to subsidize his business or industry, or to enact legislation or regulation that harms his competitors. A market entrepreneur succeeds financially by selling a newer, better, or less expensive product on the free market without any government subsidies, direct or indirect."

In the end, and it happens every time, political entrepreneurs crumble. It may take decades, but market entrepreneurs have customers on their side. I call home from Mexican vacations using Skype, which uses voice-over-IP technology to bypass the phone networks. So do an increasing number of Mexicans, for calls to and from the United States.

Subsidies inspire laziness. Lack of competition breeds sloth. Why work when you can sit back on a Mexican beach and watch the money roll in?

Phone and cellular monopolies are classic examples of political entrepreneurs at work. Thieves from the Eat People Rule.

AT&T Wireless charges 20 cents per text message, each of which is all of 160 characters. Based on the average length of texts, that comes to $5,000 per megabyte of data. Of course, no one actually pays that—as anyone with teenagers learns quickly, it is put in place to get you to fork over $10 a month or more for an unlimited texting plan. Even an expensive Internet data plan, from AT&T Wireless, no less, charges $0.005 per kilobyte or 5 cents per megabyte or, drum roll please, ten thousand times less. You think a little competition from a market entrepreneur might solve this pricing discrepancy?

Cable companies are political entrepreneurs too, with local franchise rights in exchange for fees/bribes to local municipalities. Radio and TV broadcasters? Yup. Add the water company, your electric utility, garbage collection; just about all your monthly bills go to some political entrepreneur. But you can also add anyone with a license and limited competition, usually in the guise of a geographic territory. Car dealers are classic examples. And so are liquor distributors, with laws on the books that don't allow direct sales of, say, wine by wineries. So you pay a little fee, you probably don't even notice it, but it adds up to a nice piece of change for whoever owns that franchise.

It's the market entrepreneurs that are the true heroes, honing their product or service to deliver "something of value" rather than redistributing existing wealth by demanding huge value for some trivial but government-sanctioned service. And yet, market entrepreneurs are usually cast as pirates or villains. But no matter how the general public feels about them, they win in the long run. You can be a "political entrepreneur," if you can finagle your way into it, and you may even get rich, the "easy way," but I'd sell out to some other sucker rather than milk it for very long. You sure as heck don't wait around to pass it along to your heirs.

Why? Technology changes and legislation is often written in disappearing ink. New politicians may be convinced your mandate franchise is no longer all that interesting. Good luck finding the trolley lines that used to run up and down Broadway in Manhattan.

It's political power versus competition. Over years, politics has the advantage. Over decades, competition triumphs. Cost cutting and innovation can't be caged. Choose wisely.

THIS GUY FIGURED it out—a Free Radical before it became fashionable.

Cornelius Vanderbilt was born in 1794 on Staten Island, New York. As they say about Dominicans in Major League Baseball: you don't walk off the island, you gotta hit your way off. When he was sixteen, Vanderbilt's mom gave him $100 to clear and plant an eight-acre field. Instead, Vanderbilt bought a two-mast sailboat and started charging for ferrying passengers and goods around New York. It didn't take him long to save enough to get into where the real money was: steamships. The powers that be in the New York Legislature had granted a thirty-year monopoly for steamship traffic to Robert Fulton and Robert Livingston, a classic move by political entrepreneurs. Fulton was even able to convince the politicians that he couldn't make money unless he doubled his prices. He set up a fat umbrella for Vanderbilt to shred.

In 1817, hired by a local businessman, Vanderbilt started running, quite illegally mind you, freight and passengers from Elizabeth, New Jersey, to Manhattan. He charged $1 per passenger, well under the $4 monopoly price, until he took most of the business. One dollar was probably below cost, but he also ran the ship's bar, a much higher-margin business! Vanderbilt was threatened with arrest and impounding of his ships so often that, according to Thomas DiLorenzo in his book *How Capitalism Saved America*, Vanderbilt started flying flags from his ship that said "New Jersey Must Be Free." Makes an old Jersey boy like me smile.

At one point, and how's this for twenty-first-century thinking, Vanderbilt lowered the price to zero, nothing, nada. He gave away the trip for free. He not only made money at the bar on the ship, but his wife ran a saloon at the Elizabeth port, right where the passengers conveniently spilled out of Vanderbilt's ship.

Notice, Vanderbilt didn't ask permission, he just did it. There was a $4 price umbrella and he shredded it down to $1. Fulton and Livingston eventually sued and, in 1824, the U.S. Supreme Court decided in *Gibbons v. Ogden* that interstate commerce was federal jurisdiction. So, wink, wink, only Washington could decide who could be political entrepreneurs, not states.

Vanderbilt never slowed down, charging $7 for the trip up the Hudson River to Albany, or $1 for each twenty miles for intermediate stops, well under the monopoly rate charged by the Hudson River Steamboat Association. He employed tubular boilers and coal instead of burning wood, cost-lowering innovations not previously tried by others milking the route. The competition quickly followed. Vanderbilt was eventually bought out by the Association so they could get their high fees. Over time, Vanderbilt ran one hundred ships around Long Island and up and down the coast, making a fortune.

Then he yanked the price down on the New York to San Francisco trip during the California Gold Rush. By going through Nicaragua instead of Panama, he shaved two days off the thirty-five-day trip. He cut prices from $600 to $400. His competitors were paid $500,000 by the Post Office to deliver the mail to California, so Vanderbilt offered to do it for free, and then he cut his passenger price for the trip to $150. Volume surged as every would-be gold miner had only to find $150 worth of gold to make the trip worthwhile.

It didn't take long for Vanderbilt to set his eyes on the lucrative transatlantic route. A political entrepreneur named Edward K. Collins got Congress to subsidize his business to the tune of $3 million and $1,000 a day so he could profitably run the route. Vanderbilt ran more efficient ships and undercut Collins, who was saddled with all sorts of rules and regulations that went along with his subsidy. By 1858, Collins went belly up from losing so much business to Vanderbilt. The only competitor left was Cunard, the subsidized British steamboat company. Vanderbilt cut rates, especially for second- and third-class passengers, and used iron-hulled ships with screw propellers, cutting the trip to nine days, much less than the wooden paddle-wheel boats. Again, lower prices and Scale led to innovation, even though common wisdom says the opposite, that is, we need to subsidize unprofitable business so they can afford to innovate. Yeah, right.

Again, Vanderbilt didn't ask, he just did it, lowering prices and gaining share, leaving subsidized and monopoly players in his wake.

During the Civil War, Vanderbilt sold most of his vessels to the Union and more or less moved on. Vanderbilt soon started playing with railroads, except this time he was able to buy stock, in the Harlem Line, which crossed the Harlem River into Manhattan, as well as the Hudson Line, which ran up the east bank of the river all the way up to Albany. This meant he was competing against the old Steamboat Association again, and that he could lower prices on the trip even more!

Lots of stock manipulation charges followed Vanderbilt around, and he almost lost his fortune to a competitor named Daniel Drew, in a fight over the Erie Railroad. *The New York Times* likened Vanderbilt to medieval robber barons, who as gatekeepers, or actually more of a protection racket, would charge merchants for being allowed to operate on their land without getting robbed and beaten. Robber barons didn't do anything but charge for something they could do. Historian John Steele Gordon did some work trying to find references to medieval robber barons anytime before the 1850 reference to Vanderbilt, and came up empty. It fit a narrative, though, so the *Times* went with it, but there may never have been such a creature as a robber baron. With that reference, an expression was born that is still being used today.

Vanderbilt and Rockefeller and Carnegie built giant empires by lowering costs, again and again and again, creating economic growth and increasing living standards by constantly lowering the cost for steel or oil or transportation for passengers and freight, by boat or by rail. They had scale on their side, yet they were labeled "robber barons" for amassing huge fortunes. Go figure. Find something that Scales and you'll be so lucky as to be vilified in the press and in high school history textbooks.

The real lesson? Those political entrepreneurs who thought they had it made, with a Hudson ferry, a subsidy to carry the mail, the transatlantic franchise and subsidy—they got fat, dumb, and lazy and set themselves up for a market entrepreneur to come in and take them out at the knees. Free Radicals should never rest on their laurels. Progress is a continuum. What seems like it is risk-free today carries the greatest risk tomorrow. In fact, it is the work by Free Radicals that provides the biggest risk to political entrepreneurs.

OF COURSE, VANDERBILT is long dead. But the political entrepreneur type that he took on never died. Those who milk franchises for all their worth, raising prices instead of lowering them, are alive and well. But eventually Free Radicals get them all. As soon as we find out what goes on behind closed doors.

Despite the financial mess of 2008, the United States remains the most productive country in the world. So says me, anyway. But my argument falls apart when I travel elsewhere. For example, on my trip to Paris, my cell phone worked on the Métro subway, which of course is underground. Plus, a nice electronic sign announced when the next train would arrive. Even in French I could figure that out. These signs are finally being phased in on the New York subways. It's about time.

Airports in Asia are sleek and modern, with free Wi-Fi, no less. Anyone who has waited at a baggage claim for forty minutes at JFK Airport or had their cell phone call dropped in mid-conversation or waited four hours for the cable guy to show up (and do I even have to mention the DMV?) must certainly feel that America's best days are behind us.

New York Times columnist Tom Friedman is quick to make these claims, early and often. His 2005 bestseller *The World Is Flat* described a globalization trend (that had already been in full swing for at least twenty years, in Silicon Valley) as something new and terrifying.

James Taranto picked up on a recurring Friedmanism (yes, please use that at cocktail parties): his multiple use of the expression "Jetsons to the Flintstones."

On September 30, 2007, Friedman wrote, "Fly from Zurich's ultramodern airport to La Guardia's dump. It is like flying from the Jetsons to the Flintstones."

And on May 4, 2008, he wrote, "We landed at Singapore's ultramodern airport, with free Internet portals and children's play zones throughout. We felt, as we have before, like we had just flown from the Flintstones to the Jetsons."

And on December 24, 2008, "Landing at Kennedy Airport from Hong Kong was, as I've argued before, like going from the Jetsons to the Flintstones."

And on March 3, 2010, "But, eventually, infrastructure, education and innovation policies matter. Businesses prefer to invest with the Jetsons more than the Flintstones."

I must admit, after leaving Paris, I felt the same way. I have wondered if there might be something to all that American defeatism. Until I read a series of articles in Tom Friedman's very own *New York Times* titled "A Disability Epidemic Among a Railroad's Retirees." Just from reading the first few paragraphs about the Long Island Railroad, you'll instantly understand why our public infrastructure and mass transit is Flintstonian . . . because someone is stealing the money. Cornelius Vanderbilt, who ran ships around Long Island, must be rolling over in his grave.

"Virtually every career employee—as many as 97 percent in one recent year—applies for and gets disability payments soon after retirement, a computer analysis of federal records by *The New York Times* has found. Since 2000, those records show, about a quarter of a billion dollars in federal disability money has gone to former L.I.R.R. employees."

Ouch. That's a quarter billion not spent on tracks and trains and stations and Wi-Fi or anything else. Because of the wonderful negotiating skills of the Brotherhood of Locomotive Engineers and Trainmen, these workers (classic Sponges) can retire at age fifty and get a pension that along with phony disability payments can add up to $280,000 per year. Why would you work? My back hurts just thinking about it.

And because of overtime pay and "arcane work rules, some dating back to the 1920s, which pad employee paychecks," it's even worse. "Passengers could soon face another fare increase and the transportation authority is seeking more taxpayer support, already half a billion dollars a year, to close a huge budget gap."

And this is just on Long Island in New York. A June 2010 *New York Times* story tells of a conductor earning $239,148 a year, as one of eight thousand Metropolitan Transit Authority workers earning over $100,000. Amazing.

Add to that the ever popular "prevailing wage" laws. So often, publicly managed and funded projects can cost two or three times as much to build, and take two or three times as long, as similar projects done by the private sector. California has a prevailing wage law. You would think they call around to private contractors, survey what they are paying workers in the area, and then set an average wage rate. That would make too much sense. Instead, California surveys collective bargaining agreements reached with unions, and then adds up salary and health benefits and paid leaves and disability benefits and sets a prevailing wage that can easily be 50 to 100 percent more than the local private market is paying for workers. No wonder our public works are so shabby!

What other political entrepreneurs are robbing us blind?

Well, teachers get tenure after three years and the worst of them cruise for the next thirty. Cops and firefighters all know how to game the pension and benefits system. How many times have I heard about pensions that clock in at 80 percent of the average of your last three years' pay, and the untold huge raises in workers' last three years before retirement?

California set retirement benefits in the late 1990s for the firefighters and law enforcement unions, including an option for 3 percent of salary for each year worked after age fifty. Burlingame (population 27,380) city manager Jim Nantell suggests enhanced benefits cost the city "at least $2.6 million more each year, forcing city leaders to make dramatic reductions in police, fire, library, park and recreation services."

The workers are not crooked, but if a system is set up to be milked, you take advantage of it for your own personal benefit. You would be stupid not to. But these state and local pension obligations are the noose around taxpayers' necks. Where is Vanderbilt when we need him?

It's all about incentives. An economy can increase living standards as long as the proper incentives for productivity are in place. And some sort of game theory as well to keep people honest.

A postal workers contract, dating back to the 1970s, spells out in excruciating detail how far a worker is allowed to reach when sorting mail from a bin to a cubbyhole, how long breaks should be, and so on. Sponge away. First-class mail rates, which the USPS has a monopoly in, keep going up every few years to pay for their lack of productivity, 44 cents and growing. While e-mail and BlackBerrys and instant messaging at zillicents per message have completely changed the productivity of workers, the Postal Service still exists, milking all of us for no good reason—and a $238 billion operating deficit for the USPS between now and 2020.

And it is not just government workers. The United Auto Workers has probably singlehandedly killed their golden goose. Not through high wages, although that sure didn't help. It was all through work rules. Work rules are put in place specifically to require the most workers to do the simplest of tasks. It is the exact opposite of productivity. Here's one complaint I read: "I worked in a union shop for about a year as an 'expediter.' When a panicked contractor called the factory about missing parts or screws originally ordered and supposed to be shipped with the product, I got the hot call and it was my job to remedy it. Though a bin containing 100,000 of the correct type of screws might be 8 feet from my office door, union work rules forbade me from simply grabbing them and Fedexing them in 10 minutes start to finish. Instead, I had to find the section shop steward (in a 50 acre plant), wait to present my request, wait more till he selected an appropriate union member and explained what was needed to that member, and I was not allowed to address that member directly, etc.

"The work rules turned a ten-minute task into a 1 to 3 hour ordeal! Imagine that waste of time duplicated hundreds of times per day. . . . I often wondered if we were all working for the same company. I learned that the market share of the company was a fraction of what it had once been because of product cost. . . ."

It's not bad work if you can get it. But if you're on the receiving end of this, your pocket is getting picked.

Then again, if you can make $280,000 by faking a disability, why would you even try to do anything innovative or worthwhile for society? Yabba-dabba-doo.

EVERY TIME SOME political entrepreneur lards on huge costs and jacks up prices for services (and steals wealth from the rest of us!), it opens up a window of opportunity that Free Radicals can drive a Mack truck through. Every time the Post Office raises rates for first-class mail, the faster ubiquitous electronic bill payment becomes a reality. Every time commuting prices rise, or teachers charge more for teaching less in smaller classes, a market entrepreneuring Free Radical can underprice and overdeliver, even without government sanctions. Then we all benefit, not just some narrow group.

Use Zero Marginal Cost to Create a Flood (or Someone Else Will)

"I HEARD IT. I LIKED IT. I'LL USE IT."

I never fail to say this after hearing a good story or a great joke. It doesn't cost me a thing (except a few brain cells, but those are abundant, right?) to store and deliver the same lines.

As we all know, the faster processors get and the cheaper disk drives and memory get (thank you, Scale), the easier it becomes to digitize and store things. Everybody will use it!

In effect, once my words are typed in by me or scanned in by Amazon or Google or some dude in Shanghai, they have a zero margin cost. It costs virtually nothing for someone to create another digital copy, to sell or steal or waste. I use the word *virtually* for a reason; the cost is not absolutely nothing, not quite zero, as there is some cost for storage and bandwidth and the human cost of thinking about the book or the music to copy, but for the next copy made, the costs are a rounding error, as close to zero as you can get.

What's notable is that the easiest, but certainly not the only, businesses to scale have zero marginal costs. The first working copy of Microsoft Word cost, say, $100 million to develop, but every other copy sold cost basically zero (the disk is $1, the box maybe 15 cents). The first dose of a blockbuster drug may cost $1 billion, the 100 millionth closer to $10, fully loaded, but closer to free, on the margin. The first copy of *Shrek* cost $100 million, the 100 millionth copy, especially if sold online, could be priced for no more than $1, fully loaded, as it costs basically zero on the margin to sell the next digital copy.

The key is to be able to charge for value rather than cost. That's not always obvious and certainly not always easy. And like Vanderbilt with his ferry service and railroads, don't ask, just do it. You can sort it all out later after your competitors are weakened. Like Craigslist not charging for classified listings. Just do it.

Ideas and business processes are the ultimate zero marginal cost product—you have to be creative on how you sell them. Ideas are a dime a dozen and overpriced!

My rule is simple. If you can do something with zero margin cost, do it. Because if you don't do it, someone else will.

Give it away and build some other business around it. Index it, package it, slice and dice it, write opinions on it, just don't be in the business of selling it. I like the expression: *because they can*. Someone will give a zero margin cost product or service away—because they can!

This is true of content like music and movies, but it's also true of many services. Voice calls can be free, so Skype and others made them free, only charging when they have to touch the old antiquated phone system. Skype was lucky that AT&T still charged for phone calls so they could undercut them and still charge for something.

Same for classified ads and what Craigslist did to newspapers. Classifieds could be done for free so they were, with just a $75 fee added for job listings, creating enough revenue for Craigslist to cover all their costs, and then some.

Wi-Fi and free airwaves set aside by the FCC will eventually cut into the cellular phone business. TV has high production costs but zero marginal distribution costs, beyond big amplifiers and antennas in the analog world. Yeah sure, they have over-the-air spectrum and cable channels that are their pipes. But peer-to-peer digital networks, usually out of China, are already operating under the radar screen, and pump ESPN and CNN and other channels to PCs and mobile phones. Legal suits are flying, but eventually, broadcasters won't be able to stop them, and there goes another business down to a zero marginal cost competitor.

There is a lot of hot air around free and freemiums and lots of trees will die arguing for this business model or that one when it comes to free. And don't mistake the Free in Free Radicals as part of that hot air; it just sounded cool. My message is quite simple: If it can be had for free, it will be had for free or close to free. A Free Radical shouldn't get in the way of this. Instead, use it to your advantage.

The best advice is to go upstream. I wrote about an old upstream story in my book *How We Got Here*, which incidentally was both sold and given away free off my Web site—and still is!

British clergyman and businessman Edmund Cartwright figured out that he could use cheap power from water wheels and steam engines to run looms, getting rid of the expensive people who then operated them. He knew that once Richard Arkwright's patent on cotton spinning expired, there would be a flood of producers turning out ever cheaper yarn. Yeah, yeah, not quite zero marginal cost, but thread and yarn did get so incredibly cheap the cost might as well have been zero. Not wanting to get in the way of that flood, Cartwright patented his mechanical loom "up the stack" in horizontal-speak, or perhaps better, closer to a final product than the yarn makers.

YOU WOULD THINK that words would be the first to get ripped off. Even though words and text are the easiest to copy, it's still a pain, even with the latest generation of e-readers, for many folks to actually read words on a screen instead of paper. It's more cost effective to just let some mass producer print it out in volume so you can read it via real ink. Portable readers like the Kindle are a start, the iPad is even better, and as they are much cheaper and have much better displays and proliferate in the multimillions, books will surely die. But so what? Better for readers and writers. Bad for printers and bookstores.

It was the same with music. After telephone calls, music was the next big business to be stolen digitally. You could easily listen to digital music, even if it was an entire album side length. The 1990s' rip and burn to CDs turned into the new century's rip off and download, to your iPod or anywhere else, so you could listen to it anywhere. Apple iTunes made it easy to handle music files, so they could actually charge money for something with zero marginal cost. The record labels make money from iTunes, without doing anything, no printing CDs and shipping them to stores and dealing with returns, so the digital sale had zero marginal cost.

But once the digital version was out in the wild, it became easy for anyone to copy it and listen to it. Napster file sharing turned into BitTorrent downloading and pirates ruled the high seas of music. No one knows the real numbers, but my guess is that ten times more music is acquired through piracy than purchased with iTunes.

TV shows were next. Now it's movies. And this is just the stuff that's easy to copy.

The lesson being: if someone can copy your stuff, they will, so you might as well be the one to do the copying. If it can be digitized, it can be given away. Like it or not, piracy rules.

For copyrighted things, courts are worthless. Patents are more of a brick wall—hey, they are mentioned in the U.S. Constitution, although that doesn't have much force in China or Estonia. Trade secrets are much more the way to go. If no one can figure out how you do something, you're better off.

With copyrighted stuff, even if it is illegal to copy, if it's digital, there will be an underground market for it. One huge site, The Pirate Bay, has 22 million users (and growing) searching for and finding pointers to mostly copyrighted material scattered around the Web. These "torrents" are easily downloadable, perfect digital copies of music, TV shows, movies, and as it's known on the Web, pr0n (spelling it wrong deceives profanity filters). The Pirate Bay got sued in Swedish court for "assisting in making copyright content available" and you can expect a decade of appeals.

Copyright law and its interpretations have been a mess for years. I'm always amused by pay-per-use Xerox machines in libraries, with a warning label not to copy copyrighted material—as if there was any other reason for the copier to be there. Congress was happy to pass the Sonny Bono extension to copyrights—practically written by the Walt Disney Company to protect Mickey Mouse's soon-to-expire protection—which extends artists' copyrights well beyond their deaths. Google has enflamed the anger of book authors, a dangerous group who can type faster than most, by claiming it is allowed to digitize any and all books unless the authors specifically opt out.

For the most part, Google and others hide behind a simple concept—they are in the "link serving" business. Ingenious, actually. Others violate copyrights, the argument goes, whereas these entities just serve links to other Web sites that are doing the dirty work, like hosting illegal downloads. Google just sells ads against these illegal download links. Now, that's an upstream business, closer to the final product! Google's implicit claim is that they are not the Web's police; if they were responsible for maintaining law and order, search wouldn't be nearly as lucrative a business. But aren't they in the same business as Pirate Bay?

So who are the Web's police? In the end, it's courtrooms that have no enforcement power. Swedes policing the world? Please. Courts have huge marginal costs and can't compete with zero marginal cost pirates. They don't fit the Internet model of Scalability. So really, it's no one. Like it or not, the Web is and will remain the Wild West.

Hand out as many guilty verdicts as you like, but folks on the Internet will copy away, because, really, who can stop them? Google won't do it, Internet providers like Comcast and AT&T, who can block a lot of this stuff, can't do it without network neutrality proponents squawking about interference. Even authoritarian regimes fail—the Great Firewall of China is quite leaky. Plus, it is so easy to create a Web service to download copyrighted material that if, like Whac-A-Mole, you knock one down, another five pop up in the next few nanoseconds. Sad but true: there is not much anyone can do.

So make all the legal arguments you want—no matter what court decisions are rendered and no matter what laws are passed, copyright infringement is going to happen. So music labels and movie producers should stop suing their customers or lobbying for more laws and instead come up with new business models that pirates can't follow them into. Aerosmith and Metallica have had their libraries of songs stolen, so they allow them to be incorporated into the video game Guitar Hero; millions pay for the opportunity to play along with their favorite tracks. Very high definition movies are too big, for now, to download, so Blu-ray disc sales continue to grow. As we know, iTunes is tightly linked to iPods' legitimized digital music sales. The Amazon Kindle e-book is a start, trying to kick-start a protectable electronic book platform. And newspapers and magazines need to create more than just a display bucket to webify their print words. New services—from alerts to social networking to finance to sports fan participation—need to do things paper versions can't do. Stuff that is hard if not impossible to copy and steal. Music and TV and magazine and newspaper companies are not, as they say, in the railroad/media business, they're in the transportation/communications business. It makes a difference.

As a Free Radical, you can't fight zero marginal cost. But you can sure as heck use it to your advantage.

Create Your Own Scarcity with a Virtual Pipe

So WHAT ABOUT MEDIA? IS IT WORTH ANYTHING TO FREE
Radicals? Should you have any interest all at? I'm talking about the
business of media. Should you even care? I mean, we all know that
everything is getting digitized and will end up available for free on
the Web and that all newspapers and magazines and TV stations
are headed to the dust bin of history, so why bother?

To answer that question, you really have to go back to ancient
times, say, October of 2006, when Google bought the fledgling
Web video service YouTube for $1.65 billion. Not bad for twenty
months' work by a start-up. It would have taken at least $50 to $100
million from Sequoia Capital, their venture backers, to pay for the
infrastructure and sales force to build a real company. That's real
money. You can see why they sold.

But what about Google? Why do it? And why pay so much?
Google CEO Eric Schmidt admitted in a deposition with Viacom

over copyright infringement that Google overpaid by $1 billion. $1 billion! Why?

Google is an amazing beast. Massive growth profit margins from basically one service: serving ads on pages with search results.

So why bother buying YouTube? Was this a sign of strength—"we bought them because we can turn anything into gold"—or weakness like, say, auction company eBay buying free phone connection company Skype as their auction franchise weakens. Or maybe it was desperation, such as when, in the old dot-com days, the search company Excite merged with cable modem service @Home, creating a new dinosaur from two old ones.

On the surface, Google's buy looked like a deal from strength—video is the next frontier on the Internet, etc. Face it, YouTube was a company whose amazing growth from zero to 100 million videos served per day was nothing short of spectacular. Sure, it was based on copyright infringement, amateurish video, the stomach to lose money on each video shown (that much bandwidth does add up), and a cobbled-together business model to charge record labels to show music videos, so that the world now knows that Paris Hilton can't sing. But it was a grand experiment in media. At the end of the day, Google paid up for a media property. Plain and simple.

But what does that even mean, "media property"?

Maybe it will just end up being an expensive toy for Google to play with. YouTube still barely makes money. Same for broadcasters who put their shows up on the Web, on Hulu or ABC.com—these are loss leaders while they try to figure out the right model.

Are these smart moves or just playthings? And this begs the question: What is media anymore? Who will the next moguls be?

Can Google figure it out? Can you just slap videos up on the Web and become a younger and more vibrant Rupert Murdoch or Sumner Redstone?

ACCORDING TO MY handy dandy Web dictionary (okay, answers .com), *media* is defined as: "(mē′dē-ə) Channels of communication that serve many diverse functions, such as offering a variety of entertainment with either mass or specialized appeal, communicating news and information, or displaying advertising messages."

That's pretty lame. Even Katie Couric is confused. So what is media? Like the six blind guys trying to identify the elephant, people variously think of media as content, distribution, the aggregation of attention, user-generated content, ad sales, keepers of our culture, public trust, and on and on. How can you lump TV, radio, movies, newspapers, music, cell phones, cable, satellite into one phrase?

My definition is quite simple: Media is about control of a pipe. That's it.

Done. Finis. See ya.

Everything else follows.

While media includes newspapers and magazines and even billboards, the root of practically every media empire is control of some pipe. Spectrum, bandwidth, cable lines, phone lines, sewers—any closed system.

Time Warner and Comcast: cable. Disney: TV licenses and cable stations like ESPN. News Corp.: TV licenses, cable stations, and newspapers. Even Warren Buffett got in on the game, trying to make Buffalo, New York, a one-newspaper town so he could control a pipe.

Years ago, I sat through a presentation by junk bond king Michael Milken, long released from involuntary housing for manipulating markets ("stock parking," if you want to get technical). Milken flashed some photos of his former clients: Ted Turner, John Malone, John Kluge, Rupert Murdoch, Craig McCaw. Each one of them had borrowed billions in high-yield junk debt to build their media empires. Banks wouldn't lend to them, but Milken's network would. Why? Because he saw something that banks couldn't see—each of these guys controlled a pipe to consumers, their fists gripped tightly around it, and they could leverage that control to create massive media companies.

And these weren't just any pipes, these were almost always government-mandated pipes that guaranteed ironclad control. Turner had TV station licenses, Malone had cable lines, Kluge had radio and TV spectrum, McCaw had cellular bandwidth licenses, and Murdoch, who at one time only had newspapers, bought enough TV stations to demand that regulations on ownership limits be relaxed for him to form Fox Broadcasting, challenging ABC, CBS, and NBC and their pipes. Political entrepreneurs one and all.

Ironclad? If these pipes were ones that anyone could use, there is no way Milken would have trusted these guys to generate enough cash flow to pay back his debt. He never would have lent them billions.

Nope. This is a closed system. You only allow the voices, music, or video of your choosing down your pipe. You control choice. These are metaphorically solid pipes, not flimsy PVC.

Control the pipe and you've got an economic engine to run ads against your "scarce" content, charge subscriptions, sell voice calls, and charge per minute—the world is your oyster.

Movies? Hollywood does control access to theaters—ask anyone trying to get screens for independent films—but their economics revolve around "windows," time slots to create even more scarcity, viewing movies exclusively in theaters and then moving them from pay per view to airplanes to cable such as HBO, to DVD/Blue-ray, video on demand, and eventually free TV, charging fees for each of these windows.

It's no surprise that most media companies own studios as well. Control a pipe and you can extend your business to control everything it touches—like Kurt Vonnegut's ice-nine (I'm sure some English teacher has assigned you to read *Cat's Cradle*).

ONCE YOU CONTROL a pipe, the economic model of media is pretty simple. I learned this from an old friend, Rob Hersov, who was a media banker out of London for Morgan Stanley at the time. Rob took me to meet every media company in Europe, quite a treat for someone whose media sophistication doesn't extend much beyond *Rocky and Bullwinkle*.

Over drinks in Hamburg, Germany, of all places, Rob taught me the media business model. It took all of five minutes. something he called EPI-LIT. Entertainment (or Editorial) and Perishable Information Leading Indirectly to a Transaction. All right, I know it sounds stupid, but it explains everything.

Sitcoms and sports (entertainment) along with news and weather (perishable information) draw in viewers, in whose face you jam branded advertising until they can't see straight, so they are (indirectly) led to go forth and buy lots of Bud Light, Gillette Fusion razors, Avodart, and Mazda zoom-zooms.

Rob explained to me that ad sales are based on the concept of scarcity. Yes, I now hear bells going off every time someone uses that word. And ads are an artificial Super Slopping Scarcity as well! Sellers want to reach a large and perhaps targeted audience of buyers. If these buyers are under the spell of what comes down your pipe, you can charge a premium. Weird business. The incentive is to limit the number of pipes.

And it's not just ads. Own a solid enough pipe and eventually you can control the distribution of movies, and even NFL games. TV networks bid through the nose for their football package and DirecTV charges huge fees to break the pipe so you can watch whatever game you want on Sundays through their satellite network. Another fun and circular trick is to charge high subscription fees and then overpay for must-watch sports with your new cash, which then drives more subscribers your way. As I mentioned earlier when discussing Thieves, Disney gets $2.50-plus a month for ESPN, whether you watch it or not. They then overpay for MLB baseball and NBA games, which can only be seen on ESPN. And you wonder why Manny Ramírez and LeBron James make so much. You are paying their salaries through ESPN's control of the pipe. It's a tax on the stupid (me!). We pay up for the artificial scarcity. ESPN has created some great sports programming. I watch it all the time. I just get annoyed that they use their pipe to overcharge and drive the price up for everything they touch.

Control the pipe and charge whatever you like.

Ratings allow you to charge more, but even the most unpopular shows generate decent sales. Talent eventually figured out how to weasel their way into this model, demanding huge fees per episode of a TV show or $20 million a movie in return for drawing filmgoers on opening weekend. But it's only because someone else controls the pipe that these extravagant numbers are possible.

We can't all own pipes, so this tends to leave media in the hands of a very few moguls who get Wall Street to fund their follies. They receive all sorts of praise as brilliant businessmen. These guys made a mint. But really, they're just political entrepreneurs. Big whoop. They are successful with their hands in my pocket. Not a stitch of productivity to be found. Moguls are not Free Radicals.

AND THEN THE Internet came along. Oops. Move along—no scarcity here. Cisco routers, and all the other packet-switching network equipment composing the Internet cloud ending up at that broadband router in your basement, send packets of data around to wherever folks want them—no moguls needed.

Market entrepreneurs used the chaos of that packet switching to deliver text and pictures to Web sites or phones or even TVs. Then bandwidth got cheap enough to move music around too, shattering the record labels' control of distribution. And now as bandwidth gets even cheaper and more plentiful, video starts to move around this wild packet network. Maybe those pipes are now coffins and the moguls will die within them.

The late Senator Ted Stevens famously explained that the Internet is "a series of tubes." If only that were so, moguls would continue to rule the earth. But the way the Internet actually works, there ain't no pipes to control. No end-to-end pipes, anyway.

Yeah, there are some "last mile" pipes, bringing data from the backbone of the Internet to your block, your house. Cable modems, DSL, and the spectrum used by cell phones. And yes it's annoying that media companies like Comcast and Verizon actually control a lot of the last mile, but there is still no end-to-end pipe.

Cellular is about as close as anyone has gotten to a pipe, but that stranglehold is being broken by smartphones like the iPhone that can bypass cellular networks with Wi-Fi and use apps like Skype to make long-distance phone calls a lot cheaper than AT&T and Verizon would like to charge. But even those traditional media pipes are leaky. Five- and even ten-megabit broadband into homes is now becoming standard. Wi-Fi is in homes and in Starbucks and even across some cities, providing an alternative to cellular data. Who needs to pay Comcast $99 a month anymore for cable service they don't watch anyway? Just get a data connection and off you go.

The old moguls know this too. They are all scrambling for a Web strategy.

No pipes, no moguls, no media?

GO BACK TO the Horizontal rule. The computer and voice communications businesses have transformed over the last twenty years from vertically to horizontally integrated businesses, from a pipe to a layer cake. It is 100 percent clear, to me and hopefully to you, that this is the clue as to what will happen with the mostly vertically integrated media mess.

Media companies are mostly vertical. Today it's some putz on the executive floor making decisions, swayed by internal backstabbing politics, no less. They often produce articles or shows or movies and control the outside independent companies that do. Then the media companies market them, deliver them, sell ads—everything that touches their pipe, soup to nuts, they do.

Why give up profits to those outside, blah, blah, blah.

The new horizontal model is more efficient, at least for computers and communications—with media, those leaky pipes are starting to burst. It will be fun to watch.

■   ■   ■

ONE MORE THING about the tech business being horizontal: It's not just Intel and Microsoft, which are the most lucrative and most visible winners; there are scores of horizontal slivers in disk drives, graphics, storage control, font handling, virus protection, compression, the list goes on. Same in networking and telecom. It's not just Cisco—there are stacks of useful slivers that companies can wedge their way into. The trick—and this is key—is not to pick some narrow market, but to get horizontal, go wide, serve millions or hundreds of millions of devices or users.

A bit counterintuitive, but if you think about it long enough, you'll see that if you go wide enough, you capture your share of profits while others do lots of the nasty work (like assembling PCs or iPhones, stocking shelves at Best Buy, and so on).

I can hear you thinking: how does that explain successful media companies on the Web—Google, eBay, Yahoo! (at one point), Apple, Facebook, Twitter?

Good question. Media is different from technology. You, of course, want to go as wide as you can, but you still want to control a pipe, to create some scarcity, however artificial it might be.

But where's the pipe?

No pipes. A Free Radical creates a virtual pipe.

First off, these companies are all market entrepreneurs, with almost no regulatory oversight beyond patents and copyrights, which everyone has access to. Even though the telecom cloud is a chaos of packets getting passed around and no end-to-end pipe, these companies and others have figured out how to keep content and users inside a pipe that they control. Pretty neat and quite a lucrative parlor trick.

How do you keep users in your corral? Unfortunately, that's

easier said than done. Those Internet packets go where they damn please. It's the Wild West—an open prairie. You've got to be creative. For instance, eBay created a closed community of buyers and sellers, locked in via feedback ratings, creating a layer of trust amid the chaos of anonymity on the Web. Wall Street applauded to the tune of $40 billion in market value until eBay got greedy and kept raising prices (a no-no on the Web, no?). Now eBay is struggling to show that they can grow, but they still own a virtual pipe.

There are lots of examples that work. Video game companies had a virtual pipe of sorts. They define a gaming architecture. Nintendo really perfected this in the early nineties and then sold gaming consoles at perhaps a $100 loss. They still needed a few outstanding games that would sell for close to $50. But then they allowed others like Electronic Arts to write games for their platform in exchange for rather steep royalties for the rights to run on their platform. It was a closed system. You didn't have to control distribution via retail, just what ran on your platform.

Okay, but that's a hardware example, too messy. Anything with just bits?

Sure. A slight twist to this platform strategy is Apple iTunes, a service that couples your desktop to Apple's servers in the so-called computing cloud, tunneling through the Web via a virtual pipe. If you use iTunes, you are in their pipe! If all the iPod was about was playing MP3 files, Sony or maybe Samsung would probably have owned this business long ago. But Apple created a pipe, so that in addition to all those pirated MP3 files, you could buy music or video on the Web and deliver them to your iPod or iPhone conveniently, safely, and, more important for record labels and studios, securely.

It's a pipe because music purchased on iTunes only plays on iPods and iPhones and iPads and also your PC. Using DRM, or digital rights management, Apple created a pretty ironclad pipe. With this pipe, Apple could charge actual money for songs and videos. Even if they lose money selling this stuff, they can make it up selling iPods and iPhones.

Music CDs can still be ripped—you don't actually have to buy music when piracy is a viable option. This plays to Apple's advantage—they don't have to sell you everything, just enough. Let me say it again, because it's very doable—a tight coupling between server and device is Apple's virtual pipe, tunneling right through that Internet cloud. Add their "fly like the wind" pace of new players and phone introductions and you can see why they still own this business.

Want proof Apple thinks of all this as a pipe? On June 6, 2009, Palm released the Pre, their answer to the iPhone. Palm set up the device so that it could look like an iPod or an iPhone and could instantly sync with Apple's iTunes service. On June 17, Apple announced that future releases of iTunes might "no longer provide synching functionality with non-Apple digital media players." Eat that, Palm!

How about a Web-only pipe? Who wants to deal with messy devices like game machines and iPods? Probably the earliest example of an online-only virtual pipe is instant messaging. AOL bought Israel-based Mirabilis for some $400 million bucks, whose ICQ instant messaging had millions of users and almost no revenues. Mirabilis CEO Yossi Vardi famously quipped that "revenue is a distraction." Sound familiar? Lots of new features start this way, Twitter being the latest but certainly not the last. Okay, but what really made AOL's move brilliant, an early cut at social networking, was that for a long time, instant messaging was a closed system. You had a buddy list and you went where your buddies hung out.

In the 1983 movie *Scarface*, Tony Montana (Al Pacino) explains to his buddy Manny how America (and perhaps the media) works. "In this country, you gotta make the money first. Then when you get the money, you get the power. Then when you get the power, then you get the women." Steve Case at America Online got it backwards. He had the teenage girls locked into his pipe (man, that sounds weird) but couldn't figure out how to turn it into a sustainable media empire. Instead he merged with an existing one in Time Warner and more or less killed them both.

Okay, that's still old news.

Google's got an almost $30 billion plus ad sales business. That's media, right?

Sort of. It's still more of a Web portal, albeit one done to perfection, than a virtual pipe. You go to Google to look stuff up, often before you buy something. You don't have to stay, but you do because of the relevancy of the results and how fast the results come back. Huge data centers near fast running water for cheap power and purpose-built PCs get results in 0.2 seconds, faster than they can come off your own hard drive. Other search engines are too slow. Is that it? Well, certainly some of it. Maybe the speed advantage is subliminal, but it works. Google has been piling on all sorts of fun stuff to keep you at their site. Maps are cool, Gmail is nice, but most of the rest is not really locking you in. What locks you into Google—besides their excellent and rather swift search and the billions in ads that go with it? A toolbar? Perhaps there is no lock, merely a brand backed by a technology lead. YouTube may be their quest for a lock.

Others have done it. There are virtual pipes made from scratch that lock you in, like social networking sites MySpace and Facebook, or the insanely addictive and profitable FarmVille from Zynga. But what separated these folks from the Web of old was the addition of the concept of friends, interlinks within the closed system. To have Facebook friends, you needed to be on Facebook. In April 2010, Facebook added a Like button, so that Facebook users could cruise around to other sites and identify things that they like, tagging them without having to go back to Facebook. Think about that—a Tom Sawyer move, out on the edge, extending their productive virtual pipe beyond just the borders of their own Web pages to the rest of the Web. Quite a move.

So how do you leverage these virtual pipes? Once they are captive to your pipe, you throw silly ads in front of people. Remember Rob Hersov's EPI-LIT—entertainment and perishable information leading indirectly to a transaction? Same with a twist—EPI-LIT: entertainment and perishable information leading to an impulse transaction. For the most part, it's direct advertising—create a sale, not a brand. It's a lot different game from branding beer or hair color. So far, it's been slow going. Both Face and Space have modest ad sales, mainly because of Microsoft and Google guarantees, but prices are really low. There are too many pages and most, uh, are not appropriate for an ad. Facebook is selling virtual goods, virtual currency, and virtual gifts in their virtual pipe, leveraging the Zero Marginal Cost Rule. The social network service LinkedIn stays business focused and does quite well. Going wide and controlling a pipe can sometimes conflict.

AND THAT'S JUST in the "real" world. The most amazing virtual pipe is World of Warcraft, a massively multiplayer role-playing game now owned by Activision after giving up almost half of the firm. Players enter a realm and then fight monsters and complete quests, often working with others in a guild or against other guilds. Fun and addicting.

Chew on this. Some 10 million subscribers pay $40 just to enter and then another $15 a month for access. Yup, World of Warcraft has been an amazing success: a massively multiplayer game that is easy to learn, addictive, and requires months of overuse to master to reach the highest levels to then join guilds to cruise around in packs with other like-minded WoWers. As one online poster comments, "So there are millions of people who play WoW. There are also millions of people with a drinking problem. I place them in the same category."

Talk about control—your packets do what WoW tells them to do, tunneling through the Internet cloud. Of course, the experience has to be good enough to get you there and keep you there. Add social networking—guilds of like-minded, er, adolescents of all ages to roam around and destroy things together—and you have an ironclad pipe. A view of things to come.

By 2010, Call of Duty: Modern Warfare 2 took over for WoW as the "cool" virtual place to be, to either team up with or kill your friends.

In South Korea, kids gather in "bangs" (pronounced *bongs*) to play multiplayer games. Beats hanging in front of the 7-Eleven. It's their version of WoW or CoD. I looked into how they do it. Users are locked into a front-end player, for which, again, you put up $50 for the privilege, which of course is locked into the bangs' back-end servers.

How is online gaming a business? Ads, schmads. Get your credit card out if you want to stick around. And it's addictive. Yup, this is Starbucks without cups, all fueled by 3D graphics, and now a $1 billion business. A movie with 10 million viewers is pretty good at $100 million in ticket sales, but not as profitable—a network TV show with these numbers would be replaced by Montel Williams reruns.

■ ■ ■

So WHAT IS a Free Radical to do? Moguls control pipes in a world of zero margin costs. It costs virtually zero to sell one more digital song, run one more digital ad, or post one more digital classified. As chips and bandwidth get cheaper, digital distribution eradicates the quaint old days. The time and the tools are ripe for a *go wide* approach. Especially on the Web, which, if anything, is nothing but a layer cake, many, many horizontal layers of functionality.

Let's go back to the days of so-called Web 1.0, circa 1994. There were a few online services: CompuServe, AOL, and lots of dial-up bulletin boards. The Netscape browser came along and was basically a container—a bucket. You sent out a request and the information you wanted came back in packets, which found their way from a server. This information "filled" your browser container with text and images. Browsers set off a battle between Netscape and Microsoft but, in the end, roasted the non-Web online services to a crisp.

The technology (called scripting) started to exist in 1995, but it took another five or so years for the browser to transform from a container to be filled, into a space to be programmed—you could execute code inside the browser instead of through Windows. But it wasn't until February 2005, when Jesse James Garrett defined Ajax, or Asynchronous JavaScript and XML, that a real next-generation Web was born.

Ajax was a real-time link between client and server, your computer and the cloud. With Ajax, you could run and control programs running inside the Web browser, again without hitting Refresh. Google Maps is the best example—it paints the screen with a map and then when you scroll north, the server fills in the pieces of the map you are missing.

But more important, you could do mashups—put hotel or restaurant locations into maps. Play music in your blog. Or very easily put video from another Web site into yours—YouTube uses Flash Player from Adobe. You could seamlessly link applications into each other in, dare I say, horizontal layers! This is the exactly the technology needed to create a virtual pipe.

This ability to program inside your browser allows for the "layerification" of the Web—not just transport and routers and cable modems, but applications and content too. So as the Web starts to emulate, emolliate, and eventually circumnavigate today's media, its power will come from a stack of individual layers, each a mile wide. Hence my call to go wide, own one of these many horizontal layers.

Let me say that again. It's the ability to both run programs inside the browser window and allow for applications to pass information to each other that allows media on the Web to organize into horizontal layers instead of the fat and mogul-owned pipes we are used to.

The layers are endless. Someone does search better than anyone else. Or classifieds, or music sales, or telephone calls, or video, or real-time highway traffic, or comedy, or news or social networking, gaming, recipes, or whatever anyone wants that can be delivered with zero marginal costs and provides it anywhere and everywhere. No vertical integration.

Think about how different this is from media today. The technology of sticking a microphone in front of someone, or turning on a camera or switching a phone call, was perfected years ago. It's not about technology anymore. It's about programming content, not computers, to attract viewers. With a few decent exceptions, it has been a race to the bottom.

Will a horizontal online world create a race to the top? More like higher highs and lower lows. At the edge, people pick what to do and watch according to their taste. And there is no accounting for taste. Or as Jay McInerney wrote, "taste is just a matter of taste."

But now getting packets through that bumper car of an Internet to create a virtual pipe actually takes someone writing code and designing easy-to-use services. But who wants to write code? It takes forever—Jolt, all-nighter, Nerf guns, the brightness up on the monitor and dark sunglasses to get all the bugs out. Better to let coders write code, and programmers (as in network TV) develop thirty-minute sitcoms. Layer this sucker out.

The new moguls of media will be about creating virtual pipes out of a stack of these separate layers. Want to be a Free Radical mogul? Think out all the free services never thought possible without lots of broadband and pieces you can pick and choose from to build it and you are on the right track. Twitter was built this way. No need to build a browser or even do that much work in the cloud. Just create a closed system that logged, posted to followers, and allowed for searching of 140-character messages. To tweet is to use Twitter, a now important layer in a bigger system of communications.

Unfortunately, the architecture of today's infrastructure, huge data centers near cheap electricity with racks of PCs and disk drives and uninterruptible power supplies and lots of fiber, is an artifact of our still narrowband world. It's faster to query to distant lands on fiber optic than to look something up on our own PC, or our next-door neighbor's PC. It's not zero marginal costs, not yet anyway. The more video you stream or allow users to download, the more your bandwidth and storage costs rise and the more money you lose. I've watched plenty of March Madness NCAA hoops games off of the CBS Web site. They have a long way to go to replace their broadcast and cable facilities.

But that's about to change as well. I think Peer to Peer or P2P is another game changer. It allows for true zero margin cost distribution. You download songs from your virtual neighbor. It's uploaded from their disk drive and downloaded to yours. No centralized control. It will be what starts today's media into its death flush spiral. Post-Napster music stealing sites like The Pirate Bay use Peer to Peer, using whatever BitTorrent client you might have. With P2P, video is not so much streamed as shared; you get what you need from one and preferably more than one source. BitTorrent is a former underground, now being productized version of P2P. Lots of first-run movies and TV shows can be downloaded via their "torrents," some even before they are broadcast. The Pirate Bay finds all this stuff, making it easy to find, borrow, and steal. And it is stealing, because the old media pipes are leaky.

Peer to peer is killing the old cell phone model as well, with cheap phone calls bypassing expensive phone networks. A call home from a Paris hotel lobby using Skype over the hotel's Wi-Fi was 2 cents a minute versus AT&T's $2 per minute. 100:1 gets my attention!

This is coming on fast. Pipes be gone. Video or voice or friends or location services each become another horizontal layer in this next media stack, meaning an opening for Free Radicals to take down the moguls. Hence YouTube in the hands of Google.

A lot of the complaints about YouTube and other new services are how amateurish the content seems. I'm guilty of doing this— citing dancing cats as an example. But don't be fooled by user-generated content, or as it's put down, loser-generated content. As control and intelligence moves out to the edge, professionals will eventually figure out how to leverage this new architecture.

The point of all this? New technology comes along and renders obsolete old ways of doing things. Media is not immune. Ajax and P2P are just the current examples. Mobile applications combined with GPS location information will certainly command more and more of local advertising dollars. This will change media in ways that current moguls won't like. I can only guess at the next wave of technology that will ripple through the media business. True Free Radicals will look at this as an opportunity to create their own new applications, new virtual pipes, and alter the landscape in their favor. Bring it on.

So, HOW DO you get paid when you don't control a pipe but want payments from advertisers or customers for access to that pipe? Is there an economic model to these virtual pipes? Early TV was radio shows with cameras turned on, much as early movies were Broadway shows with film running. I still fall over laughing at the Marx Brothers' *The Cocoanuts* and *Animal Crackers*, "Hooray for Captain Spaulding . . .", which were made this way. It took a while, but eventually, production values increased to $2.6 million per TV episode for *Friday Night Lights* and $100 million–plus movie budgets. This became the barrier to entry. Viewers demanded better quality, better than the cheap stuff they were initially fed. *Animal Crackers* is a classic, but now quaint.

The Web is still back in the pioneer days. Beyond the pirated stuff that leaks out of the moguls' traditional media pipes, today's Web content is mainly user-generated: MySpace pages, YouTube videos, podcasts, Facebook walls, all disgustingly cheap to produce (and armchair critics like me go sniff, sniff, and mutter "lame"). But lots of it is made and there are lots of people to view it.

I asked my friend Mark Cuban—who knows a thing or two

about both Internet video and owning media franchises, let alone the NBA and *Dancing with the Stars*—about moguls and their loss of control. He told me to watch for the eventual economic model of this whole thing as production values inevitably go up:

"Mashups, hyperlinks?" he said. "We've seen it all before in the music business. Anyone can produce and distribute any song they want. We have seen some artists and songs emerge, but very, very few. And that is in an environment where there truly are no digital barriers to entry. Yet the moguls are still the moguls. Not as strong, but still in control. I don't see them going away. Why? Because in a Long Tail universe, the cost to crawl up the tail to the rat's ass is more expensive than the production. Which means only the people with the money can make the investment, which brings you back to the moguls."

It's the Yogi Berra problem—no one goes there anymore, it's too crowded. You gotta spend as much on promotion as you do on production to attract folks to your pipe, virtual or otherwise.

Mark Cuban might be right. Moguls will still roam the earth even after the asteroid hits. But they won't be like the moguls of today. It will be a different landscape. But the view from here tells me that it won't be possible to control pipes anymore. Not like today anyway.

Programmers will create these virtual pipes. Value will be created, but I think there will be more value in the layers of technology that are needed than in the end product. New companies will emerge to leverage this architecture of layers, of P2P, of streaming through the Internet, of mesh networks for wireless last miles and on and on. You see it already with new services like Pandora and Slacker that personalize entertainment. And by knowing what people listen to and watch, Intelligence at the Edge of these virtual pipes will provide the feedback loops to constantly improve our experience, rather than the constant parade of sitcoms and stupid reality shows. These virtual pipes and how they are used will be constantly changing, unlike the copper wires and coaxial cable run to our homes that funnel the media of today.

How soon do we get there on the Web? I'm betting sooner than we all think. Moguls who whine about pirates and how silly the dancing cat YouTube videos are will get whacked in the head by a Free Radical wielding a virtual pipe. Go wide.

Money Sloshes to the Highest Returns

IF YOU TAKE ALL 12 RULES AND FIND THE NEXT BIG TREND and create the next big thing, it will require money to get going. And lots of it. Money for people, money for offices, money for computers, for labs, for bandwidth, for heat, for coffee and on and on. If you don't have enough, you need to attract it, like my Net Net example raising capital and going public. But how?

Fortunately, money sloshes around the globe seeking its highest return. To be a true Free Radical, be the highest return.

Money goes wherever it damn pleases. Moving around the globe, pulsing through electronic networks and bank databases, seeking to maximize its risk-adjusted return. Maybe someone's risk tolerance is low so they invest their money in U.S. Treasury Bills. So be it. Others (like me) think that teams of smart people inventing the future are actually less risky than big corporations that are or will soon be under attack from these entrepreneurs, so

I invest in small companies and start-ups. That's me and my money's prerogative.

Others are even more daring and invest in Estonia or the Congo or even Venezuela, places with potentially high returns but huge political or physical risks. They need to be compensated with even higher returns.

But the rule of thumb is that money will always find its way to businesses with the highest returns. That should be you.

Be productive or provide tools for others to be productive and you'll command huge profits. Money will fight for the honor of investing in your company. Don't be in a low-profit business, or else you tell the world that your products or services are useless, or of some pitifully low value. Maximizing your profits (market profits, not political profits!) means customers value your stuff. You are providing them with what they need and they are willing to pay for it. Don't get fooled by those who claim you are ripping customers off. Those profits are the price discovery markets need to see to allocate capital properly and push the boulder of progress up that steep incline.

Being the highest return also means you'll have the wherewithal to invest in future products, be able to afford the research and development dollars to keep scaling, to keep creating abundance, and keep inventing the future. It's not a forty-yard dash; it's a never-ending marathon.

You'll always have a choice of being bigger and having higher absolute profits, by selling more stuff with lower profit margins. Resist the urge. Bigger is not better. Highest returns are better.

Now, don't get me wrong. If you decide to make left-handed nostril inhalers or something with a tiny market, then highest returns aren't better. But I'm assuming you've figured out Rules 1 to 12, especially the one about Scale, and figured out that large markets serving millions and billions is the way to go.

I can't say it enough: Be the highest return.

ONE RULE OF thumb I like to use before helping start a business or invest in a business or even do any work looking into a business is FAB.

Is it a Feature, an Application, or a Business?

Entrepreneurs fall into this trap all the time. They come up with a great idea, and maybe it's just a feature. Store photos on the Internet? Flickr? Wow, that's cool. But it's just a Feature. Edit photos, share them, e-mail them to friends. Ofoto? Put enough features together and you have an Application. Now we're getting somewhere. Add words and print out two hundred holiday cards with my photo and personal greetings in it, even addressing envelopes and mailing them with my signature, like Shutterfly? Now, that's a Business. By now, all these sites have implemented this business. But being first usually helps bring the highest return.

Features will eventually be devalued, perhaps even worth nothing because of their zero marginal cost, so it's hard to generate the highest return with just a Feature. Plus, others will include your feature in their application and then you are toast. Even applications have a hard time standing alone. Ofoto was bought by Kodak in their effort to create an online business. Even if a business is not so obvious on day one—Twitter is a feature or emerging application that has a business in it somewhere—figure out what your ultimate business might be. It could change fifty times from the time you start, but don't build just features or just applications or you'll never generate the highest returns.

■ ■ ■

BUT AREN'T PROFITS greedy? Consumer backlash against profits is legendary—windfall oil profits, overpriced drugs, ESPN on premium cable. I'm the first one to get annoyed when I get charged $7 for a Coke at the ballpark, knowing all of 10 cents' worth of syrup and sugar are mixed with water and ice. Esteemed economist Navin Johnson best sums it up in the economic primer *The Jerk*, starring Steve Martin:

> NAVIN: Frosty, I'm no good at this.
>
> FROSTY: Aw come on, Navin, you're doing fine.
>
> NAVIN: I've already given away eight pencils, two hula dolls, and an ashtray and I've only taken in fifteen dollars.
>
> FROSTY: Navin, you have taken in fifteen dollars and given away fifty cents' worth of crap, which gives us a net profit of fourteen dollars and fifty cents.
>
> NAVIN: Ah! It's a profit deal!

Profit is sales minus expenses. But that doesn't tell the whole story. Wikipedia, which as a free service has mainly a societal profit, defines it as "the making of gain in business activity for the benefit of the owners of the business." But while the owner of the business makes a gain, so does the buyer, or else they wouldn't have bought the damn product in the first place.

Digging further, profit is derived from the Latin *profectus*: advance, progress, increase, growth. Hmm. Or *proficere*: to go forward, be useful.

The profit motive has been a giant carrot for centuries and is what drives innovation and productivity, which (you should know by now!) creates increased living standards and wealth.

I spent pages and pages of my book *How We Got Here* on James Watt, a University of Glasgow flunky who studied latent heat and tinkered for years until he came up with a more efficient steam engine, selling off two thirds of his future invention to venture capitalist Matthew Boulton in exchange for capital to fund his work. The whole thing was a profit deal! Watt's steam engine was originally built to pump water out of flooded mines, replacing horses that would walk around in circles running a manual pump. Boulton and Watt charged one third of the annual costs of the horses mine owners no longer needed. They all gladly, uh, ponied up. A few horses were out of a job, and a lot more miners were hired.

But Boulton and Watt plowed their profits back into scores of innovations and their steam engine ended up powering jennies and yarn pullers and looms, displacing entire villages of cottage workers, who later were employed in the very manufactories that eliminated their jobs. Say what you will about industrialization and soot and Mary Poppins chimney sweeps, the life expectancy in England doubled from 1800 to 1900 and then doubled again by 2000. Wealth from industrialization led to more specialization, better food, better medicine, better science. Yeah sure, and bizarre Victorian morals and those so-called robber barons and all the ugly mutations of concentrated wealth, but for my dollar, it beats waking up at 5 a.m. and picking artichokes.

Think of a world in which we all do each other's laundry. We all get paid, but no wealth is created. Until you get the bright idea of hooking up an ox to a wheel and invent the agitation cycle. Woohoo. You can charge less than anyone else and still make a profit. All of a sudden you own the laundry concession. Someone else owns farming or making omelets, etc. More work done, fewer people involved. An economy grows and the participants improve their standard of living, no longer washing clothes all day. This means profits for you and wealth is created. No profits, no wealth, no cancer drugs, no microbreweries, no progress. Really.

Consumers are willing to pay over cost for a product or service because it has value and is cheaper than if made or done by oneself.

But aren't profits greedy?

I circled back to my unsustainable, abundant, Bordeaux-sipping buddy George Gilder and asked him why profits aren't greedy.

I got back an earful.

"I think about profits in moral terms. They represent the index of altruism of an investment. Profits are too often seen as a reflection of greed—that's complete nonsense. Profits are just the difference between the value of a good or maybe service from the people who produced it, and the value to their customers. So it reflects the degree a business understands the real needs of their customers. That index of the altruism is the index of the orientation toward the needs of others. You can't ask for any better measure."

Of course, that's for market entrepreneurs, not political entrepreneurs with rigged profits.

He nailed it! And I suspect the greater the profit, the bigger the unfilled need taken care of. Profits mean businesses are improving the lives of individuals, while losses mean they're either doing badly by customers or they are so bad at managing their business, with no realistic plan to become profitable, that the market starves them of capital in favor of someone doing something people actually want.

And I think democracies have figured this out. Totalitarian systems rarely recognize individuals and ownership of property, so the only way to increase wealth is to steal it from someone else, bugger thy neighbor, roll tanks into Prague—geopolitical Take versus

Make. That's the fixed-pie theory of world domination. Eventually, those with productive and profitable and "increase the size of the pie" economic systems that create wealth, via a Horizontal Scalable trading model (yes, with Intelligence at the Edge Eating People!), will stop that old twentieth-century game.

I wonder if in a hundred years, some wiseass is going to tour Google's Larry Page's Palo Alto home and point out to anyone who will listen that Page wasn't really rich—what, no holodeck?

You can bet on it.

How Many?

I WOULDN'T BE SO BOLD AS TO TELL YOU THAT YOUR IDEA OR your job or your investments have to go 12 for 12 (or 13 for 13) with my Rules for Free Radicals. But the more the better.

Mark Zuckerberg's Facebook has embraced ten of the Rules; I leave it to you to figure out the ones he has missed, so far anyway.

Some Rules are easy. Jeez, if you can't find something that scales, you're clearly not looking hard enough. Finding things that are adaptive to humans—that could be a little harder. The more filters you successfully apply, the more likely that you'll find a long-run home run, something that generates wealth for decades on end, rather than some one-off one-hit wonder.

I fully admit that most of my examples and most of my filters will point to technology and electronics and information technology ideas. Biotech and genomics are fascinating fields, but there are fewer examples of scale and an edge and adapting to humans than there are with someone writing code for a mobile device or something that soon has multiple terabytes of storage. It doesn't mean that those aren't great fields for Free Radicals—it's just that I haven't been able to find things that will drive huge long-term growth. You might. Keep looking. I didn't write a book called 12 Surefire Career Ideas. I wouldn't even begin to attempt something like that. Plus, even before the ink is dry, it would be obsolete. Use the Rules to find them yourself. Things change fast and today's unknowns are tomorrow's winners. Find them first. That way you'll be the one to generate the highest returns.

And by no means are my Rules the only way to live your life and the only way to focus your career. There are lots of ways to make money, many of them challenging and personally rewarding and all that. You want to be a lawyer? Go for it. Seven years of medical school sound like fun? Be a doctor, your mother will be so proud. Insist on getting a license from the federal government to run a cell phone company or burn fuel or deliver ESPN or harvest oysters or run an auto dealership, don't let me stop you. All of them are probably decent businesses. You'll make decent money, join a country club, be a pillar of your community, be asked to join the board of the opera. Whatever. There are so many ways to make money, even a lot of money, don't let my Rules get in your way. But—there is always a but!—don't get holier than thou on me when you are driving your Prius or building huts in East Timor or donating your political entrepreneurship earnings to Habitat for Humanity or the Robin Hood Foundation or I'm Personally Saving Children/The Poor/The Planet. You may feel good about yourself, feel like you are really giving back, and maybe you just got "points for Heaven." But deep down, you know that you didn't give those gifts, the rest of us did. Through political connections, you redistributed our wealth to yourself and then for community standing or personal satisfaction, you redistributed it again to some pet cause. I'm not impressed. You could have been a Free Radical all along and improved society while you improved your own standing.

Go back to my definition of a Free Radical. A true Free Radical is someone who not only creates wealth for themselves, but at the very same time, improves the world, makes life better, and increases everyone else's standard of living. And they often pull off this parlor trick by destroying the status quo and inventing the future. Rather than being a burden on society or a stealth tax on society, a true Free Radical improves society and is paid handsomely for doing so.

It's a pretty simple test. Doctors may think they are Free Radicals; they make money and they make society better, but they do it one at a time. They don't really scale. The device maker or someone who invents an ever cheaper test to detect cancer five years earlier, now that's a Free Radical. A social worker certainly helps the poor and downtrodden, but taxpayers pay. Tort lawyers keep society safe by suing large corporations and keep them honest and focused on, for example, consumer safety. But these businesses just raise their prices and we all pay.

It's not the Servers or Sponges or Sloppers or Thieves who create progress. They are just the carriers. It's the Creators, the Free Radicals, who are increasing productivity, increasing society's wealth, reinventing the way the world works and generating enough (altruistic?) profits to reinvest in their process to keep this reinvention going for decades on end. These are the real heroes in history.

And it's by following Free Radicals, or being a Free Radical yourself, that you can find and create and leverage the next big things that make us all wealthier than some French guy whose house is now a museum.

Hackers vs. Slackers

WHILE CAMPAIGNING IN IOWA IN LATE 2003 FOR THE DEMO-
cratic presidential nomination, candidate John Edwards declared
that "there are two Americas, not one: One America that does the
work, another that reaps the reward. One America that pays the
taxes, another America that gets the tax breaks. One America—
middle-class America—whose needs Washington has long forgot-
ten, another America—narrow-interest America—whose every
wish is Washington's command." Never mind that as a class action
lawyer, Edwards was a classic Sponge and political entrepreneur—
he's ripped a page from Saul Alinsky's *Rules for Radicals* playbook,
invoking Haves versus Have-nots to scare up enough votes to get
elected. Nowhere does he talk about how wealth is created in the
first place, about productivity, or about progress. That stuff is too
complicated. So get used to it. It's never going to change. Populist
rhetoric sometimes works (it didn't for Edwards). So does paying

off voters with social programs and checks from the government. But it doesn't lead to societal wealth.

Sure, there is income inequality. We pump a trillion dollars into education and some 70 percent of high school graduates go off to college so that we lead the industrialized world in GDP at $14.2 trillion (the International Monetary Fund's 2009 numbers have the European Union in first place, where Norwegian McDonald's charge $13 for a Big Mac, but that's kind of cheating, isn't it?). And some get left behind. As a country we are far from heartless. There exists a safety net, a rather bountiful net if you ask me, with welfare and unemployment insurance and medical clinics. Yes, poverty still exists, but the way to solve poverty is not to Take more from the Haves but to create more Haves, whatever it takes.

The battle going forward is not going to be the Haves versus the Have-nots, it will be the Makes versus the Takes. Right now, the Haves are tapped. In 2007, the top 1 percent of taxpayers paid 40 percent of all federal personal income taxes. The top 10 percent paid 71 percent. The top 50 percent paid 97 percent. The Makes are already paying through the nose. And a whopping 47 percent of Takes paid no federal income tax at all (yes, yes, they paid Social Security and Medicare taxes). You're not going to tap much wealth for the Have-nots by making the top 10 percent pay 90 percent of taxes. That well has run dry. You've got to create more taxpaying Haves. So get your butt in gear and start Making productive wealth, because you are carrying a lot of other people on your back.

It's really the Hackers versus the Slackers. Not quite the typical Seattle herb-smoking, sleep all day, grunge head-banging all night slacker, but close. My use of "slacker" is more about the sense of entitlement, entitled to Take. There are large swaths of society that aren't contributing to national or worldly wealth. They might go to work every day, even do something they consider important, but they are still slacking—serving the hacker brood. And by hackers, I don't mean just the 5-Hour Energy chugging, stay up all night with the monitor brightness turned up high and wearing sunglasses debugging code hacker, although that's an important element. I mean anyone hacking away, as a Free Radical, creating productivity that increases living standards and societal wealth. This is you. Be a hacker, not a slacker.

You'll be rewarded with wealth . . . and the personal satisfaction that what you did mattered, even if no one else sees it that way.

It's more important now than ever.

There are government deficits as far as the eye can see, a sea of red ink. Debt is being laid on to distribute to Have-nots today. We need more Makes, more Hackers, more wealth creators.

I know, you know, we all know that much of that productive wealth is going to be redistributed, but don't let that discourage you. Redistribution takes many forms. Taxes and deficit spending are only the most blatant. Regulations favor the status quo and the political entrepreneur who has his hands in everyone's pockets. Environmentalism preaches a no-growth society. The word *sustainability* almost begs you to think of a fixed pie being sliced into tiny pieces—a loud and clear "no progress so let's redistribute" statement. But if you don't hack away and create productive wealth, no one will. The rest of the world is slacking.

I DON'T WASTE TOO many brain cycles on it, but I often wonder why so many people not only are antiprogress, but actively demonstrate and proselytize about their (flawed) Slacker convictions.

Sometimes I think it's about control. A free world and free market systems are chaotic. Many thrive, but in others, it upsets some inner ear natural balance and they need to grab the steering wheel and navigate the boat themselves in calmer waters. They are the Fun Suckers P. J. O'Rourke told me about, who practice bullying for weaklings. And surely jealousy plays a part. Human nature and deadly sins and all—or is it adolescence? But slowing progress in the name of jealousy is almost criminal; even jealous tendencies are a lame excuse. Self-loathing and an "I'm not worthy" attitude is probably more like it—other adolescent emotions. But then I see another, more adult, emotion—nostalgia. Ah, remember how simple life used to be. We don't need progress and financial derivatives and horizontal drilling and McMansions and fully loaded Hummers (though we'll keep the Apple iPad). Let's go back to the old days, and simpler times.

Or maybe it's a *Homo erectus* tribal instinct. Maybe we have collectivism, a "we're all in this together"/ *fraternité/égalité*, in our DNA. I had the privilege of visiting Israel with my grandfather in the 1970s as a twelve-year-old. One of the stops was an overnight stay at a kibbutz, a collectivist farming enclave. We got a tour of the facilities and a meal in their large, tourist-friendly dining room. I couldn't help but notice the waiters were all Arabs, not Israelis. Being a naïve twelve-year-old, I asked a woman who seemed to be supervising, "Doesn't everyone pitch in and wait on tables and work in the fields and clean rooms? Isn't that what a kibbutz is all about?" She looked at me, laughed, and went back to her paperwork. Stupid me. Collectivism is for idiots. I wish I had been old enough to short the Soviet Union then and there. I didn't need to read Orwell's *Animal Farm* in high school; I saw it in action.

Whatever that human trait might be, dripping in smug self-satisfaction, that defaults to a no-growth agenda, it does no one any good. We're back on Boulevard Hausmann in Paris at the rich guy's house. Actually, most of us are either working there or scratching out a meager existence to put food on the table, with no idea what great things lie ahead over the next one hundred years for our offspring. And now, so many want to stop progress dead in its tracks. There's lots of talk about environmentalism and collectivism and whole earthism and redistributionism and progressivism with not a peep about the exceptionalism that allows society to afford all the aid and social programs in the first place.

WHY IS THAT important? Because you can't just create wealth out of thin air. You can't dig it out of the ground. You can't just declare wealth ("let's pay living wages"). You can't print it with a printing press or by increasing the monetary base at the Federal Reserve. Nope—you have to invent it.

And that's where you come in.

Sure, you can join the Peace Corps or Teach for America and do your part, whatever small part that may be. You can go into public service and try to change the system. But to keep getting elected, you will inevitably fall into the same populist trap of entitlement expansion every politician falls for.

Or . . . you can make, hack, create, innovate, be productive, and multiplicate to the only thing that really matters for the future of society, and that is rolling the ball of progress up that ever steeper slope.

Do it right and you will get rich beyond your dreams. Millionaire rich, billionaire rich. You can give it away to help alleviate awful cases of poverty or misdeeds. But in making your wealth—the right market-entrepreneur way—you will have already done your share, and the share of all the slackers you carry along.

You'll be called greedy. Get over it. You'll be accused of destroying Mother Earth. Get used to it. You'll be vilified in the press for not giving enough away to the "right" causes. Get beyond it.

In the end, a Free Radical is one who carefully, consistently, and often inconspicuously pushes the state of humanity far beyond where it probably deserves to go, extending life expectancies, increasing the quality of life, and bringing more of the world's population into the developing world's grasp than any Salvation Army bell ringer, Trick or Treat for UNICEF coin box profferer, Irish gold record selling rock singer/aid demander, or whiny Nobel-winning documentary maker/scaremonger will ever be capable of.

And that Free Radical . . . is you.

INDEX